IF YOU GO . . .

One Man's Travels To Special Places
In The American Southwest
And Beyond

JOE WISE

Montrose, Colorado

© 2003 Joe Wise
All rights reserved in whole or in part.

ISBN 1-890437-88-3

Library of Congress Control Number: 2003102294

Cover and text design by Laurie Goralka Design
Cover photo: Laurie Goralka Casselberry

First Edition
Printed in the United States of America

Western Reflections Publishing Company®
219 Main Street
Montrose, CO 81401
www.westernreflectionspub.com

Also by Joe Wise

Cannibal Plateau
In The Moro
The Fish
A Sense of Place: A Century in The San Juans

For Suzanne, my traveling buddy

Preface

THIS IS NOT ANOTHER TRAVEL GUIDE. It is a series of travel essays, a travelog of trips I have made to some places which are special to me. What follows is a collection of stories I have written over the past ten years for regional and national publications such as the Travel Section of *The New York Times, Sunset, Travel Smart* and *New Mexico* magazines, the *Albuquerque Journal* and *The Santa Fe New Mexican*. I have made some notes about restaurants, accommodations, etc., but beware, some of the information is subject to change.

Table of Contents

The Million Dollar Highway 1

Rocky Mountain High Country by Car 8

Lake City, Colorado: Belle of the San Juans 14

Platoro, Colorado 18

An Insider's Santa Fe 22

The Ghosts of Galisteo Basin 32

Bland, New Mexico: A Parajito Ghost Town 37

Tent Rocks 42

Hawk Watch 45

Utah's Canyon Country by RV 50

A Costa Rican Tour at a Leisurely Pace 58

Springtime in Provence 65

For Rent: Your Own House in the Tuscan Hills 71

Florence Off Season: An Unexpected Bargain 78

Western Sicily: An Island in a Sea of Light 85

The Dolomites: The Other Italy 96

The Million Dollar Highway

DRAPED OVER THE CONTOURS of some of the most striking alpine scenery in Colorado, Highway 550 is a twisted rope of a road tethered at one end in the mountain Victoriana of Ouray and at the other along the broad boomtown streets of Silverton. Between these two scenic towns, both National Historic Districts, this energetic road climbs over the summit of 11,000-foot Red Mountain Pass, up into the mountains and back into time.

Rumor has it that the road was named for the millions of dollars of gold and silver ore plowed into the roadbed during its construction or by the woman who, after creeping across the hanging, unguarded shelf road, said she wouldn't cross that pass again for a million dollars. Those of us who love the road, now fine for auto travel, prefer to think it was named for the million dollar views it provides. In fact, it was named by the men who converted it from a wagon road to an auto road in 1923. When they totaled up their cost projections one of them was reported to have said, "Well boys, it looks like we have ourselves a million dollar highway."

Fifty miles north of Durango, the old mining town of Silverton lies plotted four-square in a narrow alpine meadow known locally as Baker's Park, the only piece of flat ground in San Juan County. Crowded close around it, oversized mountains rise abruptly from the valley at their feet and stand shoulder to shoulder in a protective arc against the sky. Few other towns can claim such a dramatic and picturesque setting.

If You Go . . .

Gold was discovered in the Silverton area in 1859, but it was not until the Utes gave up claim to the land in 1874 that the little mountain-bound town was incorporated. Prospectors streamed into Silverton and in one year staked 4,000 mining claims on the steep slopes that surround it. Sometimes the high mountain weather was so severe that one traveler, fearing he would freeze to death, came walking into town holding the tail of his donkey.

The big boom in Silverton came in 1882 with the arrival of the Denver and Rio Grande railroad, which had laid 150 miles of track in seventeen months. From that year until the boom cooled in 1918, Silverton's mines, many located above 12,000 feet, produced $65 million dollars worth of ore. In 1885 the population was 5,000 and Silverton was the only town in the United States served by four railroads. Today only the Durango and Silverton remains, one of the last two regularly scheduled narrow gauge lines in the United States.

Many things have changed since Silverton's early days when the mail was delivered on skis and Sheriff Bat Masterson rode herd on the rowdy miners tanked up at one of the town's thirty-four saloons. But wooden sidewalks still line streets that are wide enough to turn a wagon and team, and the false front buildings, many built in the 1880s, are still in use and every week the *Silverton Standard and Miner* still puts out the oldest continuously published newspaper west of the Divide.

Stay in town long enough to get a feel for the Old West. Wander the gridwork streets, numbered in one direction and named in the other for creeks and pioneers: industrialist Simon Guggenheim; John J. Crooke, inventor of tin foil; Russian immigrant-orphan Otto Mears, who criss-crossed the San Juan country with 450 miles of toll roads and later served as president of the Mack Truck Company; and a young man named K.C. Gillette who, after nicking his straight razor, invented the disposable blade.

Have a chocolate malt at the soda fountain in the drugstore on Green Street. Stop in for a drink at the mahogany bar in the 1882 Grand Imperial Hotel. Don't miss the San Juan County Museum and the monument at the courthouse that tells the story of Silverton's mines. Shop for rocks and curios. Take a jeep trip over the breathtaking 12,000-foot Alpine Loop. And leave time for a round trip on Durango and Silverton railroad, still puffing its way through the forty-five miles of scenic Animas River canyon.

At Silverton, the Million Dollar Highway, one of the most spectacular automobile roads in Colorado, begins its climb over 11,000-foot Red Mountain Pass to Ouray. Opened as a toll road in 1883 to serve the booming mining districts, this road, built using only horses and men, is a marvel of engineering. Amazed at the feat, the editor of the *Solid Muldoon* noted on making his first trip, that the grade of the road "is four parts vertical and one part perpendicular and is dangerous even for pedestrians."

Climbing and twisting for twenty-six miles up through the historic Red Mountain Mining District, the road is lined with mines that honeycomb the area, mines with names like Yankee Girl, Orphan Boy, Silver Bell and Paymaster, whose numerous sun-browned wooden skeletons are postmortem reminders of the area's mineral wealth.

On both sides of the road ochre mine dumps stain the hillsides. Crisp brown mine buildings and cabins the color of Lincoln Logs, their backs broken by the weight of too many winters, cling precariously to the steep slopes. Fireweed and Queen Anne's lace bloom in the roadside ditches, and lording over it all, the vivid presence of Red Mountain, its bare top the color of masa flour streaked with Chimayo chili.

The road tops out at a breathless 11,118 feet, eye-level with mountaintops sculpted by glaciers into vast cathedrals of broken horns and cirques. From the parking area at the crest of the pass, seductive trails lead up to the mountains' summits and secret places. Here you will find those for whom being in the mountains is as important as being near the sea is for others. It is the preposition that is important. Being in the mountains means being surrounded by the mountains, physically and spiritually, dominated by their presence and their majesty, pleased by their infinite variety and mercilessly confronted by feelings of personal insignificance, as if summoned to the court of a powerful and magnificent monarch.

Leaving the summit, the road curves north down past the cinnamon remnants of ghost towns and stage stops to the head of the

If You Go . . .

Uncompahgre Canyon where Bear Creek Falls passes under the road and plunges 225 feet into the river below. Here is the site of the original tollgate — five dollars for a four-horse stage, two dollars for a single rider and horse. Beyond the tollgate site, the shelf road bends around a high rock ledge and out of sight.

Chiseled and blasted from the sheer cliff face, the narrow road hangs over the Uncompahgre River hundreds of feet below. Old photos show barely enough room for one team of horses to travel along the rocky ledge. The road is wider now, and the original grade of twenty one percent has been tamed to six percent but the guardrails are gone, abandoned when the road was opened in the winter to allow for more efficient plowing.

Rounding a broad curve, the road, which had been in such a hurry to leave the timberline, hesitates at the top of a ladder-like series of switchbacks long enough to afford a view of the glacial Uncompahgre River valley and the town site of Ouray, appropriately dubbed the "Switzerland of America." Wedged into a dead-end box canyon a quarter mile in width and a mile in length and surrounded by peaks that rise halfway to the vertical, there is barely enough room along the river for the painted order of the little wooden town.

In 1875, prospectors spilling over from Silverton came in search of silver on the slopes that surround this natural amphitheater. One of the largest mines was Camp Bird, an operation so prosperous that the sinks in the miner's boarding house were topped with marble.

The five-mile jeep road to the mine leaves the highway just south of town and climbs straight up the mountain to timberline. It is not a trip for the faint hearted, but well worth it for those who want a glimpse of the past and an unparalleled view across the corrugated roof of the Rockies. In nearby Yankee Boy Basin, famous among calendar photographers, late summer wildflowers litter the ground of this alpine meadow like colorful confetti.

Ouray is charming and well kept. Its wide streets are lined with Victorian buildings that appear to have been painted the day before. Many serve as headquarters for the tourists who use the town as a center for jeep trips, horseback riding and mountain hikes.

Check out the Ouray County Museum for a display of the area's mining history. Browse the crowded aisles of the Buckskin Booksellers for original Western artifacts and the best book selection in the area. Fish in some of the area's many streams and lakes, hike to Cascade Falls, and then watch the sunset while you soak away the strains in the soothing waters of Ouray's historic outdoor hot springs.

For those of us who can't seem to get the mountains out of our system, the San Juan country is a mecca and the Million Dollar Highway is the temple within it. But it isn't only the tempting topography of the mountains that stirs us. As much as their wildness and their bulk, what intrigues us about mountains is the way they have determined history, the effect they have had on the men who spent their lives struggling against inclines and gravity, and it is that satisfaction as much as anything that brings us back.

The Million Dollar Highway takes you through a fierce, stark and uncompromisingly beautiful place. It is a stunning trip anytime, but especially in the fall when the snows of late September dust the mountaintops with white and the aspen trees put on their saffron show.

If you go . . .

SILVERTON

Where to Stay
▲ **Villa Dallavalle Bed & Breakfast.** 1257 Blair Street. On the Historic Register, this old inn has seven rooms, each with bath, tastefully decorated in Silverton western theme.

Where to Eat
▲ **Handlebars Restaurant and Saloon.** 117 E. 13th Street. Old West dining room with fireplace and bar serves steaks, ribs and hamburgers for lunch and dinner.

If You Go . . .

▲ **The Pickle Barrel Foods and Spirits.** 1304 Green Street. Pleasant café food for breakfast, lunch and dinner.

What To See and Do
▲ Durango and Silverton Narrow Gauge Railroad offers round trips to Durango four times a day (970-387-5416).
▲ Jeep Tours over the scenic 13,000 Alpine Loop to Lake City. San Juan Back Country Tours (970-387-5565).
▲ Summer events include George Bernard Shaw festival at the old Miner's Union Theater (970-387-5337), Silverton Jubilee Music Festival, Great Rocky Mountain Brass Band festival.
▲ For further information: Silverton Chamber of Commerce (800-752-4494).

OURAY

Where to Stay
▲ **China Clipper.** 525 2nd Street. This distinctive three-story inn on a quiet side street near the center of town features bay windows, balconies and a full width veranda. All rooms have private baths, some with fireplaces, outside entrances and decks. (800-315-0565).
▲ **Historic Western Hotel.** 210 7th Avenue. Built as a miner's palace, this 1891 hotel features period furnished rooms, tin ceilings, stained glass windows and a western bar (888-624-8403).
▲ **Box Canyon Lodge & Hot Springs.** 45 3rd Avenue. Thirty-eight rooms with mountain views, some with fireplaces. Mineral springs hot tubs are terraced on the mountainside adjacent to the building (800-325-4981).

▲ **Christmas House Bed & Breakfast.** Five luxury guest suites with private baths and mountain views in a charming nineteenth century house (888-325-XMAS).

Where to Eat
▲ **The Outlaw Steakhouse.** 610 Main Street. Recommended by *National Geographic Traveler* and *The New York Times*, this rustic downtown restaurant features good food, one of the best bars in the West and a hat that belonged to John Wayne.
▲ **Cecilia's.** 630 Main Street. Affordable family dining featuring a wide selection of home-style meals including homemade soups and pies.

What To See and Do
▲ Guides to the foursquare block walking tour of Ouray history are available at the Chamber of Commerce (800-228-1876).
▲ Jeep rentals and tours are available from Switzerland of America Tours (970-325-4484) and San Juan Scenic Jeep Tours (970-325-4444) for those who want to experience the high majesty of the mountains and the mystery of their ghost towns and mining camps.
▲ Tour the Bachelor-Syracuse Mine and pan for your own gold (970-325-0220).
▲ Ouray Livery Barn offers mountain trail horseback rides (970-325-4606). Mountain biking and hiking opportunities are unlimited.
▲ Summer activities include Victorian House Tours, Ouray Chamber Concert Series, the Culinary Art Show and, for the more vigorous, the Imogene Mountain Run over the divide to Telluride.
▲ For further information: Ouray Chamber of Commerce (800-228-1876).

Rocky Mountain High Country By Car

FROM SANTA FE, IT'S LESS THAN HALF A DAY'S DRIVE to the highest automobile pass in the United States. Built in 1880 as a toll road to supply the mining camp of Aspen fifty miles away, Cottonwood Pass, now paved to its 12,126-foot summit, serves modern-day sightseers and travelers seeking a scenic shortcut from the southern Rockies' eastern slope into the Taylor River valley and to Gunnison beyond. With the 1882 opening of Independence Pass twenty miles to the north, Cottonwood Pass fell into disuse until it was reopened for auto travel in the 1950s.

Beginning at the traffic light in the center of Buena Vista, Colorado, highway C.R. 1306 (Main Street) heads due west into the spectacular Collegiate Range made up of Mounts Harvard, Princeton and Yale. All over 14,000 feet, these massive peaks were named by Ivy League students working with Frederick Hayden, who surveyed the southern Rockies in the summers of 1874 and 1875.

Six miles west of Buena Vista is the site of Harvard City. Now reduced to three buildings, this once-prosperous mining camp, established in 1874, also served as a major outfitting and supply center for miners and freighters in the area until 1882.

Beyond Harvard City, the road follows Middle Cottonwood Creek before leaving the valley to climb through eighteen miles of some of the most striking alpine scenery in the Rockies. Ascending in order though pine, aspen and spruce forests, the pass tops out astride the Continental Divide at 12,126 feet. From the small parking area on the summit there is a panoramic view of the ragged bulk of the Elk Range stretched out across the horizon to the west.

Mats of wildflowers bloom on the rocky ground above timberline. Paintbrush, columbine and rockwort spring from every niche. Marmots sun themselves on the rockslides, their warning whistles lost in the thin air.

The pavement ends at the summit, but the gravel road on the back side of the pass is well maintained and wide enough for two cars. On the ten-mile descent, the blue water of Taylor Reservoir is visible through the trees 4,000 feet below.

A left turn in the broad, sage-brushed Taylor River valley leads to the mining town of Tin Cup. It is said to have been named in 1860 by James Taylor, one of the first prospectors in the area. Searching for a stray horse, Taylor noticed some "color" in the sand of a dry creek bed and brought a sample back to camp in his tin cup. When he washed the sand, he found gold in the bottom of the pan.

Tin Cup prospered and at its peak in 1882 had a dozen stores and shops, several hotels, twenty saloons and boasted as population of 6,000. Water was piped into town and fireplugs stood on every corner. Many of the houses were elegantly furnished, and one had a tennis court.

Drawn by the smell of money, gamblers, outlaws and bunko artists swarmed to the town to separate the miners from their newfound wealth. Dance halls and gambling houses were running day and night. There were so many gunfights, that the cemetery had a Boot Hill division for those who "died gloriously or otherwise in the thick of smoke from guns."

In 1917, after years of dwindling production, the last mine closed and Tin Cup went from boom town to ghost town. In the 1950s, the few cabins that remained were being rented to fishermen and hunters. Now rediscovered, Tin Cup has been resurrected as a rustic retreat for vacationers from the flatlands, who come for the scenery and the mountain air.

Beyond Tin Cup's wide meadow, the road begins its climb south to the 12,000-foot summit of Cumberland Pass. Rising quickly

If You Go . . .

from its course along the streambed, the road breaks suddenly out of the trees into a vast bare rocky cirque bounded by broad, gray peaks. The barren bowl is so large it is impossible to judge the distance. Ahead, the shelf road, cut into the side of the steep slope, stretches out in a thin white scratch angling upward toward the rim.

At the top of the pass, a small rectangle of almost flat ground marks the summit nearly three miles above the sea. In all directions, broken, stained peaks and deep valleys fall away steeply to the tender pastels of the distance.

A series of switchbacks lead down off the summit and into the trees. Just below timberline are the ruins of the Bon Ton Mine, once a rich molybdenum mine, nothing of its glory left now except the wooden skeleton of a mill and the cinnamon remnants of cabins, roofless and overgrown, tilted against the incline that threatens them.

Ten miles farther down Quartz Creek is the town of Pitkin where, from its beginning in 1879, mines such as the Nest Egg, the Silver Age and the Silent Friend produced millions of dollars of silver ore. Pitkin's boom began for real on the morning of July 15, 1882, when the Denver, South Park & Pacific's first passenger train arrived through the newly completed Alpine Tunnel a few miles northeast of town. The arrival of the railroad opened country that was previously accessible only by high mountain passes closed eight months of the year.

An astounding feat of engineering, the Alpine Tunnel crossed the Continental Divide at 11,523 feet, the highest adhesion railroad (not cog) in the world. In the race against William Jackson Palmer and his Denver & Rio Grande railroad to the valuable coal deposits in Crested Butte, Jay Gould and his Denver, South Park & Pacific had taken a desperate gamble. Instead of going around the mountains, they would go through them.

The route west led west from the Arkansas Valley near Buena Vista up Chalk Creek to an 11,000-foot ridge where they could climb no further. With no other option, on January 8, 1880, South Park's engineers bored into the slide rock and decomposing granite that formed the shoulder of Altman Mountain. It was a decision that contributed to the ultimate failure of the South Park line.

Working at high elevations, the workers faced driving winds, temperatures that fell to forty degrees below zero, and blizzards that left snow drifts forty-feet high. The project, which was to have taken six months, took eighteen. More than 10,000 men worked on the tunnel for varying periods of time. Many quit after only a few days.

When it was completed at a cost of $300,000 in 1882 dollars, the 2,500-foot long tunnel contained 1,500,000 feet of timbering and was lined with 500,000 feet of California redwood.

But in the end, the grand dream failed. Buffeted by the strong competition and the high cost of keeping the tunnel open in the face of snowdrifts and avalanches, the South Park finally gave up. The train that passed through the tunnel on November 10, 1919, was the last.

A nice side trip is the fifteen-mile drive from Pitkin to the west portal of the tunnel in Alpine Gulch at an altitude of 11,500 feet. The road follows the old railroad grade and, while rough in spots, is negotiable by car in good weather.

For those who want to see this unspoiled alpine world, for those who would see this land as their forefathers saw it, before the paved roads and the power lines, before we got at it with what we call progress, the road over Cottonwood and Cumberland Passes is a godsend, and the fact that you can see it by car puts it within the reach of most of us.

If you go . . .

Allow all day for the trip. Spend the night in Buena Vista and start early. Afternoon thunderstorms are frequent in the summer months and can spoil the views. Start the trip from Buena Vista — the morning light is better going west. Dress in layers. The temperature can change quickly at high altitude. Take a picnic or stop for lunch at the café in Tin Cup. If you have car trouble, there are other travelers who can help you. Gasoline is available in Tin Cup. A polarizing filter for your camera will improve the quality of your high altitude photographs.

If You Go . . .

BUENA VISTA
Where To Stay
▲ **Alpine Lodge.** A classic 1950s motel with twenty, well kept, knotty pine paneled rooms two miles south of town near the intersection of U.S. Highways 24 and 285 (719-395-2415).
▲ **Adobe Inn.** An historic bed and breakfast with five rooms on U.S. 24 downtown (719-395-6340).
▲ **Vista Inn.** A new forty-one room motel on U.S. 24 near the center of town (719-395-8009).

Where To Eat
▲ **Casa del Sol.** Downtown on U.S. 24. A charming restored log and adobe miner's cabin with seasonal patio, featuring good chili dishes.
▲ **River Valley Inn.** Downtown on U.S. 24. Full menu family-style dining featuring homemade soups and deserts.

GUNNISON
Where To Stay
▲ **Best Western Tomichi Village.** A forty-nine-room motel with all the trimmings on a landscaped setting one-mile east of town on U.S. 50 (800-641-1131).
▲ **Waterwheel Inn.** A two-story building with fifty-two rooms located on park-like property along the Gunnison River 2.5 miles west of town on U.S. 50 (970-641-1650).
▲ **Hylander Inn.** A well-kept motel with twenty-three rooms on Tomichi Avenue adjacent to Western State College campus and Legion Park. Added attraction: Just across the street from Daylite Donuts (970-641-0700).

Where to Eat
▲ **The Trough.** Varied menu including fresh trout and wild game 2.5 miles west of town on U.S. 50.

For more information contact the Buena Vista Chamber of Commerce at 719-395-6612 or the Gunnison Chamber of Commerce at 800-274-7580.

Lake City, Colorado
Belle of the San Juans

LAKE CITY IS THE ONLY TOWN on the only paved road in Hinsdale County. Not so much preserved as spared, it is stranded in the heart of the San Juan Mountain wilderness where time and history left it when the miners who made it famous walked off the job in 1893.

To be sure, many things have changed since its heyday as the Queen City of the San Juans. The dirt streets have been paved, running water and indoor plumbing have replaced the washbasin and the thunder jug. And trucks now deliver the supplies that once arrived, accompanied by the metallic music of trace chains, in heavily laden wagons.

But the same cottonwoods still shade the same chinked log cabins and Victorian houses and still arch, their upper branches almost touching, over the same wide streets. And shoppers, now in Jeeps and Chevy Suburbans find what they need in the same painted false-fronts on the single row of businesses across from the park, and in the evenings after dark, stars still dangle just out of reach and the air is still fragrant with the smoky incense of wood stoves.

Wedged into a cozy river valley 9,500 feet above sea level, Lake City is surrounded by sky-scraping alpine peaks and 20,000 square miles of national forest. There is barely room enough in the valley for the painted order of the little wooden town. At its widest point, from the eroded breccia cliffs along the river to the talus slope behind Bluff Street, Lake City's neat rectangular grid work is only five blocks wide. A walker who didn't stop to talk could travel the length of it from the Henson Creek bridge to the AMOCO station in less than five minutes, and having reached the carseat bench by the door of the station could very nearly see, while resting there, both city limit signs.

Lake City's charming mountain Victoriana has been preserved by the good fortune of its inaccessibility and the foresight of its 144 year-round residents who have secured its designation as a National Historic District. Its 125-year old history is well represented by numerous examples of charming and well-preserved period architecture and the comprehensive exhibits of western mountain Americana at the Hinsdale County Museum.

In addition to turn-of-the-century ambiance, the traveler who happens on this little mountain gem will find much to reward him. For the sportsman, three lakes and thirty miles of mountain streams are home to rainbow, brown and brook trout and there is first-class fishing from baseball's All Star break until the frosts of October turn the aspen to saffron glory.

Perhaps foremost among Lake City's attractions is the alpine scenery, which is both spectacular and accessible. The Alpine Loop, a well-maintained jeep road, is a thirty-mile circuit through some of the most breathtaking mountain scenery in the United States. A drive over this once-busy stagecoach road gives the modern traveler a feel for what this fabled backcountry-mining district must have been like 125 years ago when hordes of strike-it-rich prospectors poured in seeking their Golden Fleece.

Beginning at Lake City, the road ascends Henson Creek canyon to appropriately named Oh! Point, the summit of 12,800-foot Engineer Pass, from which you can look down in awe on the corrugated roof of the world. Along the canyon, the road passes the trail head for hikes to Uncompahgre, Wetterhorn, Red Cloud and Sunshine Peaks and numerous abandoned mines that dot the area, including the cinnamon remnants of the Ute-Ulay, where once the Italian Consulate was called in to negotiate with striking Italian miners.

From the Engineer summit, side roads lead to Ouray and Silverton, easy day trips. The main road descends to Animas Forks, once a booming mine town, now derelict, and for a while home to Thomas Walsh, who some say was one of the star-crossed owners of

If You Go . . .

the Hope Diamond. His bay-windowed two-story house still stands on a rise above town.

Beyond Animas Forks the road winds up a series of hairpin turns along the back side of Cinnamon Pass to its dramatic 12,600-foot summit, the apex of a radial drainage area that gives rise to the headwaters of the Uncompahgre, Gunnison and San Juan Rivers. Just over the summit, near the ruins of the Tobasco Mine, look for the turn off into American Basin. In this natural amphitheater, open to the north and shaded by surrounding peaks for all but the middle of the day, the protected snowpack melts slowly, and the runoff keeps the valley floor moist all summer, conditions perfect for the high altitude wildflowers that thrive there covering the ground like colorful quilts.

After passing down through the abandoned town sites of Tellurium, Whitecross, Burrows Park and Sherman, the road enters the valley of the Lake Fork of the Gunnison River just at the mouth of Wager Gulch, where a side road turns up a narrow canyon back into the mountains. Four arduous miles away, the road ends at Carson City, a nearly complete and well-preserved ghost town sitting astride the Continental Divide at a breathless 11,000 feet. A hotel, several log cabins and a stable, timeworn and sun-dried the color of gingersnaps, wait in the meadow like a forgotten Western movie set.

No visit to Lake City would be complete without a trip to Windy Point, a roadside lookout halfway up Slumgullion Pass. From here there is an unobstructed 180-degree view of the Swiss-like, 14,000-foot Uncompahgre Range west of town.

Returning to town, you will pass the six-whitewashed posts that mark the Packer Massacre site and the graves of the five men who are buried there. The Packer Massacre is the local legend in Lake City and has been since that summer day in 1874 when a reporter from *Harper's Weekly*, traveling with a crew surveying a road through the wilderness valley, wandered onto an abandoned campsite where he found the remnants of the five men's mutilated and rotting bodies.

Alfred Packer, guide for and sole survivor of the ill-fated prospecting expedition, was convicted of murdering his five companions and living off their bodies during the remainder of the severe winter that had trapped them. The gravesite just south of town at the foot of Cannibal Plateau is a regular stop for summer tourists.

"Lake City is just about as close to heaven as a man can get," says Perk Vickers, owner and operator of Vickers Dude Ranch. "My Dad came here on horseback in 1888 from the coal mines over at Crested Butte and we've had this ranch ever since." Once a working ranch, it was converted to a guest ranch by Vickers' father who built cabins in the 1940s to capitalize on the postwar, car-borne tourist boom.

The individual cabins, each made from hand-hewn spruce logs and chinked with cement, are thoughtfully spaced along the river that runs through the ranch. Each of the cabins has its own porch that commands a view of the river valley and the oversized mountains that stand shoulder to shoulder in a protective arc against the sky.

"The old house was up in the high pasture, but Dad wanted it down close to the road so the tourists could see it. So he brought down an old window frame and carried it around looking through it till he found the view he liked and he put the house right there."

A visit to Lake City is a giant step back in time. For those who are preoccupied with the past, for those who, for whatever romantic personal reasons, yearn to see things as they might have been, for those who nurture in themselves the notion that it is possible to reach back across time, Lake City is as welcome a discovery as a potsherd or a pit house.

If you go . . .

▲ Contact Lake City Chamber of Commerce, 800-569-1874

Platoro, Colorado

DRAPED OVER THE MOUNTAINS that lie piled along the New Mexico-Colorado border, the southern San Juan Wilderness area contains thousands of miles of unspoiled alpine terrain including 13,000-foot Conejos Peak. It's one of those rare places where you can take a car into that special high country above the timberline.

From Chama, New Mexico, Highway 17 leads up into these mountains and back into time. Climbing north, the road labors over 10,022-foot Cumbres Pass accompanied most of the way by the tracks of the Cumbres & Toltec Railroad. Built in the 1880s to serve the mining towns of the southern San Juans, this little narrow-gauge train, looking much as it did in the days of Butch Cassidy, is one of the last remnants of the Denver & Rio Grande Railway that once crisscrossed the mountain West, shipping gold ore out and civilization in. Lucky travelers will get a glimpse of this little train puffing along on its daily trip between Chama and Antonito, Colorado.

Just beyond the summit of the pass is the turnoff for the wilderness area and the tiny town of Platoro, the area's solitary settlement and site of one of the oldest mining camps in the district. The road leads up a glacial valley climbing for twenty-six miles along the headwaters of the Conejos River, matching it turn for turn. The dirt road is sometimes rough, but easily managed in a standard two-wheel drive car. At the head of the valley, hemmed in by peaks still snow-patched in the summer, the buildings of the little wooden town sit browning in the sun.

Platoro, Colorado

Platoro, as the name might suggest, is not actually flat. Its glacial valley, cut into the high flanks of Conejos Peak by the weight of twenty centuries of packed blue ice, slopes, but not steeply considering its location nearly 10,000 feet above sea level. But everything is relative, and for the prospectors who named it, men who spent their lives struggling against inclines and gravity, it was the most nearly level ground around.

In its heyday, when rich gold and silver ore were being shipped from its mines, Platoro boasted a population of 300. One mine, the Mammoth, was bankrolled by a cardshark partner who left for the gambling tables in the valley when operating funds ran short. After a second boom in 1902, the ore played out and the miners left the valley to the river and the grass. In the 1950s, Platoro was rediscovered by a small new breed of prospector, attracted this time not by the gold in the hills, but by the hills themselves. Seeking the silence and the scenery, these newcomers restored the old cabins that still make up the foursquare grid work of the little town plot.

In addition to the private cabins, two lodges offer room and meals for visitors and there are a number of campsites in the area. There is plenty of space for hiking and biking and horseback riding, and there's still enough quiet to just kick back and watch the day wear itself out against the sky.

Fishermen come to fish the clear waters of the Conejos River that winds through the valley, or the reservoir two miles above town. Trapped in a rocky canyon, the many arms of this blue reservoir look less like a lake than a place to explore in a canoe, and its icy waters are home to lake trout and salmon.

North of Platoro, the road climbs through fifteen miles of spectacular mountain scenery, over a series of high passes, along rushing streams and through empty alpine meadows perfect for a picnic. Deer graze without fear in the undisturbed land where traffic is so light that we saw only a few cars on the trip.

Cresting a ridge after a series of switchbacks, the road flattens out on a hummocky highland at a breathless 12,000 feet at the site of appropriately named Summitville. Along one side of the broad

If You Go . . .

meadow is the dump for the Annie and Old Adams mines. Lining the other side of the meadow is a row of listing and weather-beaten cabins, once home to the miners before the ore failed and they walked off the job fifty years ago.

Discovered in 1870, the mines of Summitville were, by 1883, the largest gold producers in Colorado. At its peak, the population of Summitville was more than 1,500. In addition to the cabins for the miners, buildings included two hotels and fourteen saloons, most of which have come down under the snow of too many winters.

There is no mining now. The ore is low grade and current prices can't support the work. A few men continue the drainage and reclamation work, but on the day we were there, the yellow equipment was silent. We picnicked in the cool sunshine on ground so littered with wildflowers — penstemon, yellow Indian paintbrush, purple fringe — it was not possible to step without crushing them We walked among the cabins, now hollow-eyed and empty, where men must have dreamed of riches. Standing in the eerie quiet of the meadow, once filled with the sounds of hope and industry, I thought I could hear, as if it were real, the measured rhythmic song of the hammer and drill.

Beyond Summitville, the roads run off the mountains through the wilderness area like the radial drainage of the watershed. To the south, the road joins Alamosa Creek and chases it to La Jara. To the northeast, the road crosses the high saddle of 13,180-foot Bennett Peak and follows Los Pinos Creek to Del Norte. Not willing to give up on the day, I took the long way home, down the Forest Service road descending along Park Creek to join U.S. 160 just west of South Fork.

Next time I go to Platoro, I'm taking my fly rod. The trip from Sante Fe takes only about four hours, which leaves plenty of daylight to check into the lodge and be on the river in time for the evening hatch. I'll spend an evening or two on that good-looking water meandering through the meadows just below town. And I'll probably go to Summitville again, just to stand again in one of those special places where mountains and history come together. And next time, I'm taking the road home over Bennett Peak. I want to see the top of just one more mountain.

If you go . . .

Where to Stay
▲ **The Lodge at Platoro.** Provides rustic lodging and meals. During the summer, the Lodge offers fly fishing seminars under the direction of Thomas Peña. 719-376-2321.
▲ **Skyline Lodge.** Offers a variety of accommodations and meals 719-376-2226

An Insider's Santa Fe

CLIMATE, CULTURE AND CUISINE HAVE COMBINED to keep Santa Fe on the short list of U.S. tourist destinations. With 300 days of sunshine, moderate temperatures and humidity always in the heavenly range, Santa Fe is perfect for both outdoor activists and those who prefer its laid-back ambiance.

Founded in 1610 as La Villa Real de la Santa Fe Francisco de Asis, ten years before the Pilgrims landed at Plymouth Rock, Santa Fe is the nation's oldest state capital. The city fathers, determined to preserve the romantic image of the city, used building codes to insure the Pueblo Revival architectural style. As a result, downtown Santa Fe, with its low-profile adobe buildings laid out four-square around a shaded plaza, still has the look and feel of the Pueblo Indian culture that preceded it.

Compact and walkable, this Old World town is crowded with galleries, museums and shops. It might surprise the practical traveler to learn that it is possible to enjoy the varied delights of the City Different without ringing up a budget-busting credit card balance.

Although Santa Fe does not have an airport for commercial jet traffic (residents don't want the noise), nine major airlines serve Albuquerque International Airport, an easy fifty miles to the south, and the competition spawns some good rates. United Airlines flies daily prop commuter service to Santa Fe from Denver.

Rental cars are available at both airports, but because Santa Fe is so temptingly walkable, you can skip that expense. Pocket the savings and take a cab from the Santa Fe airport, or the Sandia Shuttle that leaves the Albuquerque airport every hour and drops you off in the center of Santa Fe at the Hilton hotel. Reservations are required.

If you do rent a car in Albuquerque, skip the interstate and take the back road to Santa Fe (State Highway 14) along the Turquoise Trail, through the time-worn mining towns of Cerrillos and Madrid. The Trading Post at Cerrillos and the Mine Shaft Tavern at Madrid are worth the stop. Tip: After joining I-25, take the Old Pecos Trail exit for the scenic route into Santa Fe. Avoid Cerrillos Road with its strip malls and motels.

A trip to Santa Fe should begin with a walking tour of the historically rich city, once the homeland of the Pueblo Indians, capital of the Spanish American empire and the terminus of the Old Santa Fe Trail. After a visit to the museum in the Palace of the Governors on the Plaza, the tour winds through adobe alleys and walled streets stamped everywhere with the history of hundreds of years and three cultures. The tour ends at the Plaza, with its cottonwoods and white wrought-iron benches, still a perfect place to while away the time reading or people watching.

History buffs should stop by the Tully House just off the Plaza and pick up a copy of the Historic Santa Fe Foundation's *Old Santa Fe Today* which includes maps and photos and descriptions of fifty historic sites within walking distance of the Plaza. For an insider's look at some of Santa Fe's private homes and gardens, take one of the tours provided by Behind Adobe Walls conducted weekly during July and August.

Many tourists come to Santa Fe just for the museums. The flagship of the New Mexico museum system is the Palace of the Governors, built on the Plaza in 1610 as the original capitol of New Mexico. Here, permanent exhibits portray four centuries of Hispanic and American history in New Mexico, from the Spanish conquest to the Santa Fe Trail to the present. Within the palace building are two excellent museum shops, the bookstore with one of the Southwest's best collection of books on art, history and anthropology, and the print shop and bindery which offers limited-edition works produced on a hand operated press.

If You Go . . .

Across the street from the Palace of the Governors, the Museum of Fine Art's permanent collection includes more than 8,000 regional works including those by Georgia O'Keeffe, R.C. Gorman and the Taos masters. A museum shop sells prints and books about art of the Southwest.

At a second museum complex three miles form the Plaza just off Old Pecos Trail is the Museum of Indian Arts and Culture. One of America's leading institutions in the study and interpretation of Native American culture, it was founded in 1931 by John D. Rockefeller, Jr. Interpretive displays portray historic and contemporary lifestyles of Pueblo, Navajo and Apache culture, including more than 50,000 pieces of jewelry, pottery, baskets, clothing and rugs. A new 14,500 square-foot wing houses the museum's new permanent collection, *Here, Now and Always,* which showcases more than 1,500 objects and is narrated by the voices of Native American writers and scholars. Regular demonstrations featuring traditional tribal skills including weaving, music and dancing are conducted in a seventy-seat multimedia theater.

Adjacent to the Museum of Indian Arts and Culture is the Museum of International Folk Art. This unusual museum features 130,000 objects from more than one hundred countries and includes toys, costumes, sculptures and textiles. Particularly popular are the dioramas of miniatures, people of the world at work and play.

Although not part of the New Mexico museum system, the Wheelwright Museum of the American Indian is also located at the museum complex. Founded in 1837 by Boston scholar Mary Cabot Wheelwright in collaboration with a Navajo medicine man, the building resembles a Navajo hogan with an east-facing doorway and traditional interlocking log ceiling. The collection features the arts of all Native American cultures and includes rotating displays of jewelry, silver, pottery, baskets, paintings and rugs. In the basement, the Case Trading Post is an arts and crafts shop built to resemble a turn-of-the-century trading post. An outdoor sculpture garden includes works of Allan Houser.

Perhaps the showpiece of Santa Fe's museums is the recently completed Georgia O'Keeffe Museum. Its permanent collection of

O'Keeffe's works includes many of her paintings, watercolors, and drawings, pastels and sculptures.

For a week each August the world's largest and finest Indian Market fills the Plaza with the work of Indian artisans from all over the United States. Smaller in scale than the Indian Market, but equally attractive, the Spanish Market features articles with a Spanish Colonial flavor.

Shops around the Plaza are hard to beat for quantity and variety, especially if you are in the market for Indian jewelry, pottery or rugs. Indians still market their wares each day under the portal of the Palace of the Governors and the prices are right. If you leave the Plaza to shop, check out the bargains at Tin-Nee-Ann Trading Post.

Santa Fe's biggest shopping bargain is located seven miles north of town next to the Santa Fe opera. Open every weekend, the Flea Market is filled with the booths of fifty to seventy-five traders offering everything you can get in town from turquoise to Talavera. A round trip taxi fare from the Plaza is about $25, but you may save more than enough to cover your fare. If you drive, stop for lunch or dinner at the Tesuque Market on the way back to town. The food is good and the market is frequented by the glitterati.

For the art lover, no trip to Santa Fe would be complete without a foray up Canyon Road, two blocks east of the Plaza. Tucked into the corners along this narrow street are most of the area's 170 galleries, open every day except Thanksgiving and Christmas. The Friday evening stroll to the galleries' art openings is a Santa Fe tradition.

Save some time for just poking around. Santa Fe is that kind of place. Wander the walled adobe streets. Browse the bookshops. Search out the courtyards and cafes. Find the surprises.

Santa Fe's climate is perfectly suited to the usual outdoor activities including tennis and golf, both available at public facilities. For the more adventurous, there are horseback rides and white-water rafting trips down the Rio Grande canyon.

From downtown Santa Fe, it's only a thirty-minute drive to the alpine forests of the 12,000-foot Sangre de Cristo Mountains. Within the four wilderness areas that surround Santa Fe, there are more than

If You Go . . .

1,000 miles of hiking trails, many suitable for mountain biking. Maps are available at the Convention and Visitor's Bureau in the Sweeney Convention Center. To get a feel for the area, try the Glorieta Ghost Town Trail, perhaps the loveliest hike around. This gentle 3.5-miler meanders through ponderosa forests and meadows and is a showplace for wildflowers. Pick up a copy of *Sierra Club's Day Hikes* in the Santa Fe Area.

Sunny Western skiing is only twenty minutes from town, with thirty-eight trails and 1,700 feet of vertical drop, lift lines barely long enough to catch your breath and daily lift tickets still under forty bucks. Round-trip bus rides are available from downtown.

Regular bus tours include Taos and the prehistoric cave dwellings at Bandelier National Monument. Visits by car to the eight northern pueblos, the Puye Cliffs and the Pecos Pueblo ruin are all within an easy day trip. For a special treat, take the full moon night walk at Pecos ruin.

If you drive to Taos, be sure to return on the High Road (State Highway 518) through the mountain villages of Penasco, Trampas and Truchas where a European Spanish dialect is still spoken. Near the turn-off to the High Road is Rancho de Taos with the most photogenic church in New Mexico — especially when the morning light floods its face. Leave time for the famous weaving shops in Chimayo and for dinner at Rancho de Chimayo, an old adobe hacienda.

Taos Pueblo is everything you expect, hauntingly similar to William Henry Jackson's 1870 photograph. Not so for the other northern pueblos. The best pottery is at Santa Clara, San Ildefonso and San Juan pueblos, but be prepared for government housing.

Lodging in Santa Fe can be a bargain. At least a dozen bed and breakfasts — many within easy walking distance of the Plaza — have charming rooms for as little as $65 a night.

Casa de la Cuma has seven Southwestern style rooms and romantic casitas that offer affordable luxury in the heart of Santa Fe. Grant Corner Inn, a perennial favorite half a block from the Georgia O' Keeffe Museum has twelve rooms. Water Street Inn is a cozy adobe warren near the Plaza. El Rey Motel, everybody's favorite motel for two generations, has old New Mexico white stucco style, swimming pool and four acres of landscaped gardens. You won't feel like you are in the city.

Downtown hotels, such as the Eldorado and the Inn of the Anasazi tend to be a bit pricey. La Fonda is an historic and perhaps the most reasonable downtown hotel, has a comfortable leather, wood and tile Old World ambiance. It has the added advantage of being at Santa Fe's epicenter on the Plaza and its Bell Tower Bar, the highest place in town, is a great place to watch the sunset. La Posada is a romantic collection of low-profile casitas— each unique and many with kiva fireplaces — nestled village-like on six acres of shaded ground two blocks east of the Plaza.

Santa Fe is, above all else, a food town. The telephone book lists 227 restaurants and cafes — one for every 200 residents. Some are four- and five-star dazzlers, but many are quite reasonably priced with lists of entrees around $10. The wide variety of culinary choices range from northern New Mexico-style stacked blue corn enchiladas and green chili stew to Continental to imaginative nouvelle cuisine as good as it gets. Try the wines made in New Mexico, the oldest wine-making region in the United States, Gruuet's champagne is a delightful surprise.

The Shed is hard to beat for classic New Mexican food. The place to recommend if you only have one choice, this comfortable old restaurant occupies several rooms and the outdoor patio of a rambling hacienda built in 1662. The green chili stew and the green chili corn chowder are local favorites. Tip: The Shed is very popular. Reservations are taken for dinner only. For lunch, be prepared to wait with a drink in the patio.

Tia Sophia's is a wooden-boothed favorite with the locals for breakfast and lunch. Enchiladas, chorizo omelets, breakfast burritos and the Blue Plate Specials are all worth a try.

Dave's Not Here, with the best chilis rellenos in town, have kept natives filling this tiny café for ten years. Tomasita's, across the river at the picturesque old Santa Fe Station, is the restaurant most recommended to travelers by the locals for classic northern New Mexico fare and the best sopaipillas in town. At least one morning skip

If You Go . . .

the B & B bran muffins and go to Tecolote for the best breakfast in New Mexico. Huevos rancheros and pancakes with piñon nuts are the standbys, as well as the chicken livers Tecolote — sautéed chicken livers with spicy salsa and fried eggs.

For the ultimate in Santa Fe takeout, enroll in the Santa Fe School of Cooking and master New Mexico cuisine for yourself.

Some of the tastiest meals in town are served at Whistling Moon, a quirky Mediterranean bistro a short walk from the Plaza. Start with falafel with tahini. My favorite — the fafta burger, spiced lamb sausage on rosemary focaccia. Be sure to get the coriander-cumin fries for yourself or you will be eating off your dinner partner's plate. Pranzo is the place for both solid and innovative Italian. Start with the frito misto — fried calamari, shrimp and scallops in a spicy tomato sauce — and move on to the duck and wild mushroom mascarpone ravioli. Pranzo has great deserts and the best coffee in town. Ask for a table on the popular rooftop terrace. Julian's, with its candlelight and kiva fireplaces, is the most romantic restaurant in town. Specialties include Tuscan cuisine. Try the melannzane alla griglia con pepperoni and the addictive petto di pollo in agro dolce. Ask for a table in the small room to the right of the door. Pastability, this insider's favorite in the Design Center, is a mama/papa run red-checkered cucina where dinner music is provided by an accordionist on roller blades. The menu changes every day and everything is good.

Cowgirl Hall of Fame serves open pit barbeque, steaks and Cajun specialties that are worth the short walk down Guadalupe Street. Their Western Americana bar is classic. If you are there for dinner, stay for the music. Café Pasqual's, perhaps Santa Fe's most eclectic restaurant, is famous for its breakfast of huevos motulenos — a combination of blue corn tortillas with eggs, black beans, goat cheese, fried bananas and homemade red chili. The baked Brie and garlic dinner appetizer is a showstopper. For some interesting dinner companions, ask for a seat at the community table. Reservations are essential.

Café Paris in Burro Alley is a prize. If I had one meal to splurge on, it would be at this cozy little charmer that serves the best French food in town. Reservations are a must for this Santa

Favorite. You can throw a dart at the menu and be pleased with the selection, but whatever you have for an entrée, start with the mussels. The venerable Compound, Santacafe and the Inn of the Anasizi Restaurant are too "swell" for my taste but there are too many other choices.

The Five and Dime general Store on the Plaza sells Frito pie, Santa Fe's quintessential dish. Eat it on a park bench in the Plaza across the street. Harry's Road House on the Old Las Vegas Highway is ten minutes from the Plaza. This place is funky, even by Santa Fe standards. You can sit at the counter with the locals or at one of the mismatched, painted tables. I have never been by there — morning, noon or night — that the parking lot was not packed. It features imaginative entrees and comfort food. Half the choices every day are specials with seasonal ingredients, and it is THE place for dessert.

Don't leave town without having a green chili cheeseburger at Santa Fe landmark Bert's Burger Bowl. ("Since 1939. One location, worldwide").

For an afternoon snack, go to the French Bakery in the La Fonda. Have coffee and an empanada in the sun at the Downtown Subscription, or a civilized tea in front of the fireplace at the Hotel St. Francis.

For the best bars try Coyote Café, a colorful, noisy rooftop cantina. You can't see the sunset, but the airy bar overlooks town and is great for people watching. The outdoor Bell Tower Bar at the La Fonda has a drop-dead sunset view. The Ore House has a second-story veranda overlooking the Plaza. The bar at the hotel at the Hotel St. Francis has dark wood paneling and a fireplace and a European feel. Hotel Plaza Real Bar, my favorite, is just quiet and old and intimate with only a few tables and cushioned benches. It's a bar where you can actually have a conversation.

Vanessie's is Santa Fe's most popular piano bar. No cover and the menu is good enough to stay for dinner. The best nights at the Fiesta Lounge at the La Fonda are Wednesdays and Thursdays when loveable veterans Bill and Bonnie Hearne play the country classics. Lots of boot-scootin' Texas two-step.

If You Go . . .

Santa Fe After Dark
Some rank the Santa Fe Opera behind only the Metropolitan Opera. Performances are staged in a stunningly redesigned open-air amphitheater on a wooded hilltop seven miles from town. The nine-week season, which features a mix of European classics and American premiers of twentieth-century works, runs from the first week in July through the last week in August.

From August to May, the sixty-piece Santa Fe Symphony presents classical and popular works at evening and matinee performances. A pre-concert lecture precedes each performance. Each summer, the Santa Fe Chamber Music Festival offers fifty concerts featuring international artists. Santa Fe Pro Musica's chamber ensemble performs September through May in the beautifully restored turn-of-the-century Lensic Theater.

For a complete guide to the area's entertainment, pick up a copy of "Pasatiempo" in the Friday edition of the *Santa Fe New Mexican* newspaper.

Special Events
During the first weekend after Labor Day, the Fiesta de Santa Fe is a four-day citywide celebration a la Mardi Gras culminating with the burning of a forty-foot tall effigy of Zozobra, "Old Man Gloom." The Rodeo de Santa Fe is a genuine, bronk-bustin' old-fashioned outdoor rodeo held the second week in July.

Santa Fe is not only the oldest state capital, but at 7,000 feet above sea level, it is also the highest. Prepare to dress in layers. Day and night temperatures can vary as much as forty degrees. Summer daytime temperatures average eighty-five degrees; nighttime temperatures and nights average twenty to thirty degrees. Although daytime temperatures are moderate, the sunlight is intense. Bring a hat and sunscreen. Tip: Allow for an easy day or two after arrival to adjust to the altitude.

Santa Fe is a delight any time of year. Personally, I encourage you to come to Santa Fe in the winter, preferably at Christmas, when crowds are gone, the prices are down and the farolita-lit town is at its dressed-up best. And for the winter visitor, perhaps the best reward of all is waking up to those seamless blue skies and sunshine on the wrinkled gingerbread of old adobe frosted with new snow.

If you go . . .

Getting Around
Taxis are available and reasonable. Bus fare is fifty cents between points within the city. Schedules are available on each bus. Street-side parking is scarce during the summer months. Use one of the fifteen city owned parking lots in the downtown area.

Odds and Ends
Bring comfortable walking shoes. Men will not need a tie. A bolo tie is good anywhere. If you don't have one, they make good souvenirs. Photographers take note — Santa Fe's legendary hard, clear light, vivid color and bold shadowed contrast are ideal for both color and black-and-white photography. Santa Fe is a safe town for tourists. Biggest risk is theft from your car. Lock it!

For Further Information
▲ Accommodation Hotline 800-358-6879.
▲ Write for a Santa Fe Visitor's Guide 1440-A St. Francis Drive, Santa Fe, NM 87505.
▲ Sandia Shuttle Reservations: 505-474-5696.
▲ Santa Fe Web Site http://www.santafe.org.

The Ghosts of Galisteo Basin
San Cristobol Pueblo & Comanche Gap

THE DRIVE FROM SANTA FE SOUTHEAST to the Galisteo Basin takes less than an hour, but it is a trip that takes the traveler back in time a thousand years. Empty and quiet now except for the ravens and the wind, this lonesome plain was once home to 10,000 people. By 1700 A.D. they had vanished like prairie smoke, leaving behind the tumbled remains of ten large pueblos and panels of mysterious rock art.

It is thought that these early people of the Galisteo Basin survived under marginal circumstances until they were driven out by successive raids by invaders from the plains of what is now northern Texas. The remains of their pueblos, in part because of their number and large size, are a priceless natural treasure rivaling Mesa Verde and Chaco Canyon.

Much of the Galisteo Basin is now private property so to see this special place I joined a small tour of the basin organized by the Museum of Indian Arts and Culture guided by the Curator of Anthropology, Curt Schaafsma. We rendezvoused in the parking lot of the church in Galisteo where we transferred to three vans for the day-long trip.

Our first stop was at San Cristobal, or Yam-p-ham-ba (a narrow strip of willows) was built in 1300 and is thought to be the only pueblo in the basin to survive the Spanish period. Following the Pueblo Revolt in 1680, San Cristobal's last inhabitants probably migrated to the other pueblos along the Rio Grande, some as far away as the Hopi mesas in Arizona.

The Ghosts of Galisteo Basin

The site of San Cristobal lies just below a rocky bluff on the banks of a creek where it flows out of the hills and into the broad basin. In addition to hiding a number of painted caves and sacred places, the bluff provided a vantage point to watch for raiders from the plains to the east.

The pueblo, now reduced to a gridwork of rock ridges, is overgrown with the summer cypress that thrives on the pueblo ruins and marks them clearly, even at a distance. At one time, San Cristobal was one of the largest pueblos in the Southwest, four or five stories high and containing as many as 600 ground floor rooms. From the pattern of the fallen walls, it is still possible to make out the arrangement of the room blocks, plazas and kivas of this once grand pueblo.

We walked among the remnants of the old walls where pottery shards littered the ground like confetti. Curt discussed the characteristics of several pieces, being careful to replace each one exactly as it had been found. I picked up a piece of black-on-white biscuit ware and turned the shard in my hand, feeling the cool smoothness. On the inner side was a single fingerprint in the fired clay. My mind leaped the 700-year gap like a spark to the sunny morning when the hand that left the print had formed the pot.

The original pueblo, its remnants much harder to make out now, was built on the south bank of the creek and may have housed as many as 1,000 people. Sometime after 1400 A.D., the inhabitants built a new pueblo on the north side of the creek, abandoning the old one.

San Cristobal was the first site in the Galisteo Basin to be excavated. Using the then-new stratographic excavation technique in which the dirt is examined layer by layer, a chronology of settlement events could, for the first time, be established with some confidence.

Just up the hill from the pueblo are the ruins of the Spanish mission built in 1620. Standing beside the stacked order of its remaining walls, I was reminded that when the pilgrims stepped ashore at Plymouth Rock, Spanish priests were already giving thanks here in chapels beamed and lit.

If You Go . . .

In the rock cliffs behind the ruin, there is a haunting array of cave paintings and petroglyphs. Thought to have been created between 1300 and 1680 A.D., the compelling artifacts represent examples of what is called the Rio Grande style — kachina masks, horned serpents, cloud terraces and shields. Some of the figures — four-legged animals, stick figures, birds, flute players and hand prints — are in the Anasazi style, as seen on the Colorado Plateau, and are thought to be much older. Some simple geometric designs might have been left by hunter-gatherers as early as 1 A.D. The remarkable ceiling of one of the caves is painted black and decorated with stars.

Many cultural changes took place in the Galisteo Basin about 1300 A.D. The changes included, not only the influx of the Anasazi from the Colorado Plateau, but also the appearance of a new social order. This new order, the Kachina culture, transcended the traditional clan loyalties and provided the social structure and cultural glue that allowed the clans to put aside their individual loyalties and, for the first time, live together in large communities. The leader in this new social order was not the clan leader, but the Kachina leader, and villages could grow large without dissolving into intraclan squabbles. This period that gave rise to the large pueblos.

The Spanish brought a new religion which the Indians initially adopted along with their own. But by the early 1600s, the Indians had begun to lose faith in this new religion and the priests tried to stamp out the competing "heathen way," a campaign that included burning thousands of Kachina masks and artifacts. This oppression sowed the seeds of resentment that led to the Pueblo Revolt of 1680 when the Spanish were chased from New Mexico. Following their return, a second Pueblo revolt in 1696 failed, or the Spanish might have been thrown out for good.

From San Cristobal, we drove south across the basin, stopping to climb the fortress-like volcanic mesa that was the site of Pueblo Largo from 1200 to 1500 A.D. Now reduced to a cross-hatched network of rock rubble, this pueblo contained nearly 500 ground floor rooms. Nearby, archeologists have discovered a number of kivas and pit houses that predate the pueblo.

The Ghosts of Galisteo Basin

A mile to the west, we stopped at the base of a rock-strewn cliff where great slabs of sandstone have fallen from the face of the white bluffs. Chipped on the face of these natural galleries are hundreds of petroglyphs, including one of the most remarkable in the basin, a large warrior figure and shield.

Among the other characteristic images appearing in the basin around 1300 was the horned serpent, often decorated with a checkerboard collar. This image can be traced to Mexico and a culture that believed the earth was a flat crust of land floating on a great body of water. The horned serpent ruled the water, allowing it to come to the surface through springs and lakes and streams. It also allowed mist to rise from the tops of the mountains where it then coalesced into rain for the crops. Worshipers pacified the serpent who, if annoyed, would writhe about causing earthquakes and floods.

Further around the base of the bluff is the site of Pueblo Colorado, or Tze-man Tu-o (place of the eagle's claw). Here are the red sandstone remnants of eleven room blocks, many thought to have been multistoried. Established around 1200, the pueblo is thought to have been destroyed by raiders from the plains of northern Texas.

Looking out over the remains of the old city's intricate geometry, it is easy to imagine the walls still standing and, within them, pointed ladders and painted pots. That on flat rooftops strips of meat hang drying in the sun, that women still sing over their metates and bronzed men trade turquoise for colored feathers in the dusty shade of the plazas.

We climbed the talus slope behind the pueblo to inspect a ceremonial cave high on the face of the cliff. Using binoculars, we could see inside the cave a series of red masks painted on the cave walls. Below us and to the south the basin stretched away into the tender pastels of the distance like a tight, tan drum head, trimmed only with the green braid of cottonwoods along the arroyo. Caravans of cumulus clouds moved across the horizon on the wind and, stretched out beneath them, our next destination, the black volcanic dike of Comanche Gap.

IF YOU GO . . .

This striking landform presents a natural barrier through which raiders from the plains would have had to pass. Here, thousands of petroglyphs pecked into the rocks and cliff faces present one of the finest displays of rock art in the West. The images present a typical array of Rio Grande style rock art including kachina masks, ceremonial figures and cloud terraces as well as birds and animals. In addition, there are many war symbols such as shields and shield-bearing warriors, horned figures, four-pointed stars and bears.

Unlike other examples of rock art in the basin, this display is not near any of the pueblo sites. This fact, plus the large number and prominence of warrior images, has suggested that this natural passage from the plains may have been decorated to advertise the warrior culture in an attempt to frighten away intruders from the plains.

And the discoveries continue. In 1990, archeologists working ahead of road crews widening U.S. 285, found an ancient site with fifteen pit houses, several storage pits, two kivas and forty human burials. Many of the skeletons had signs of head and arm injuries that may have occurred in battle. Tree ring dating of the pit house beams indicate the structures were built as early as 1200, perhaps by seasonal hunters.

Five rolls of film later, we left the basin, our minds filled with questions and our cameras filled with images of star gods and warriors. At the local spa I soaked away my strains in the soothing hot waters, then treated myself to a gourmet meal at the Galisteo Inn. After dinner, reluctant to give up on the night, I sat for a while marveling at the same bright stars that turned so long ago over the heads of those primitive artists and builders. All in all, it had been a good day.

IF YOU GO . . .

 Each spring and fall the Curator of Archeology at the Museum of Indian Arts and Culture, leads a tour of rock art sites at Comanche Gap followed by a visit to Pueblo Largo and Pueblo Colorado. For more information, contact the Museum of Indian Arts and Culture at 505-476-1258.

Bland, New Mexico
A Parajito Ghost Town

IN A NARROW CANYON at the end of a dirt road high on the wooded flank of the Jemez Mountains, three weathered buildings struggling against time and gravity mark the site of what was once one of the boomingest mining towns in New Mexico.

The three buildings, sun-dried and baked the color of gingersnaps, are all that is left of Bland, a once-prosperous town that, in its heyday, boasted a population of 3,000. Founded in 1894 after several gold and silver claims were established in the area, the new boomtown soon became known as Bland, named for congressman and presidential nominee, Richard Parks ("Silver Dick") Bland of Missouri, whose Bland-Allison Act of 1878 helped prop up the falling price of silver.

Miners from all over the Rockies poured in to the area known as the "new Cripple Creek," and scattered claims grew rapidly into a group of fifty producing mines. The town grew so fast that it was said that a resident of the town, after two weeks absence, would not recognize it on his return. Four sawmills and 100 men working day and night couldn't meet the demand for lumber, and additional material had to be hauled in by stagecoach. In one four-month period alone, more than fifty houses and businesses were built.

At its peak, Bland had squeezed into its sixty-foot-wide canyon two banks, a hotel, the *Bland Herald* newspaper, an opera house and a stock exchange, in addition to boarding houses, schools, saloons, gambling halls and a red-light district. There was even some talk of building a church.

If You Go . . .

When the narrow canyon was filled with buildings, enterprising residents blasted and dug deep holes into the steep slopes to serve as their homes. One main street owner was forced to put his outhouse in front of his home because there wasn't room for it elsewhere.

Electric power to run the mill to light the town was carried on thirty-five miles of power lines strung up the canyon from Madrid. Some of the old poles can still be seen in the canyon. Water was piped in from adjacent Medio Dia Canyon, a canyon so deep and so narrow that the sun could be seen only at midday.

Over at Albermarle, Bland's sister city, mines lined the main street. Ore was hauled over an electric tramway to a 175-ton-per-day stamp mill, the first all-steel structure in the state. A three-and-a-half mile wagon road known as the "Teamster's Nightmare" linked the two towns across a high bridge. One section, where the rugged track climbed 1,500 feet in less than a mile, was the site of some spectacular accidents, with wagons and teams sometimes plunging into the canyon below.

The town boomed during the late 1880s and the early 1900s. The first gold and silver strikes were assayed at twenty dollars a ton. During Bland's raucous career, ore valued at more than a $1 million — $150 million in present-day money — was taken from the nearby hillsides. But in time, costs rose and the quality of the ore played out. The mines at Bland collapsed in 1903, along with a general decline of mining in the West. Few people stayed on. The post office closed in 1935 and by 1950, Bland was a ghost town.

As I walked from the gate up the hill to the town site, the only ghost I saw that day was the smiling, Casper-like caretaker named Wayne, who lives there year-round.

"It's a good thing I'm here," he said, as we walked the main street, "or they would carry off the place, like they have done over at Albermarle. Nothing left there but foundations. Once I found two guys up there with a moving van."

We walked the hillsides above town, once clear-cut for timber and firewood, now covered with eighty years of second-growth forest. Scattered through the woods, the stone foundation of houses, overgrown with pine and potentilla, lay in their rocky niches. We passed a cinnamon cabin listing into the hillside that threatened it.

"A man named Hofheinz lived here," Wayne said, as we scrambled over the steep slopes. "He did all the stonework for the town."

We looked inside the roofless jail that had been cut into the hillside and lined with stone, the barred windows still in place.

"The shackles were in here 'til a year ago," Wayne said, " 'til somebody stole 'em."

Along the main street, the site of the bakery is overgrown with oaks and underbrush. Dandelions bloom in the chinks of the closely fit masonry of the storage room wall, the dark interior still cool in the summer afternoon. Next door, two remaining stonewalls of the bank, closed off with a cedar-post fence, now serve as a makeshift corral.

We crossed the street and entered the parlor of the Exchange Hotel. On a bookshelf, along with back issues of the *Bland Herald,* is the original leather-bound hotel register. At the top of the first page is this entry:

Mrs. Thos. H. Benson, Prop.
Guests without luggage are required to pay in advance

The hotel opened on June 15, 1899, and the first guest was Frank Botsford of San Diego. During the first two months, the hotel was host to sixty-five guests registered from Santa Fe, St. Louis, Chicago, New York, Washington, D.C., Cripple Creek, Sonora, Mexico and British Guiana.

Behind the parlor is a dining room and a large kitchen with a twin-oven cookstove. Upstairs, thirteen wainscoted guest rooms with antique wooden bedsteads line the narrow hall.

The saloon next door is filled with boxes of old books and magazines including the January 1911 issue of *National Geographic,* yellowed copies of *The Graphic* and *Matilda Ziegler's Braille Magazine* for the blind. Makeshift shelves are lined with old bottles, purpled by time, and empty cans of Revolution Smoking Mixture ("It's mild and

If You Go . . .

mellow") and cans that once held Embassy, ABC and Canadian Ace beer. A propane-fired Coldspot refrigerator hums in the back corner. "It freezes everything," Wayne said.

On the other side of the hotel in the double bay-windowed doctor's office, the walls of the bedroom are papered with pictures from magazines, and in the medicine chest are bottles of Salcion tablets and a jar of Ben Gay spelled the French way, Ben-Gue.

Sitting the on the hotel porch in the cool sunshine awash in the perfume of the sun-warmed pine planking, I turned to Wayne.

"What's the best thing about living up here?"

"Peace and quiet," he said without hesitating.

"What's the worst thing?"

"Winter. It's a sixteen-mile round-trip to the nearest store. That's a long way to go on skis for a beer."

Too bad, I thought. If it were 1894, he could have had a beer at one of the dozen saloons in town.

As I drove down the canyon from the past toward the city, I stopped by the ruins of the old stamp mill, collapsed except for its rock chimney, standing like a headstone. For me, people in the mountains were a problem I had never completely resolved. Somehow, it was all right for the prospectors and miners to have been there. It was as if they were a part of the country like the rocks themselves. It was as if history had begun with them.

It is a romantic notion, I know. I knew that the miners had abused the country. I have seen the pictures, the photographs of the shaft houses, the trams, the dumps. But their scars on the land had healed. The timbered slopes they had stripped to stump-bare had re-grown, the smoke from their mill fires had cleared away, their trash had decomposed. The reality of their offenses was gone. Their careless, muddy tracks in the garden were overgrown.

Near the ruined mill was the entrance to a small mine where someone's dreams had soared, and died. Once filled with the sounds of hope and industry, the shaded canyon is quiet now. Birdsong, and the wind in the trees have replaced the song of the hammer and drill.

BLAND, NEW MEXICO

IF YOU GO . . .

 Bland is now on private property. Please respect it. If you want to visit, check with Helen Blunt, who works at the convenience store in Cochiti Lake.

Tent Rocks

THOSE WHO LOVE LANDFORMS will love New Mexico's newest national monument. Just forty miles from the Santa Fe Plaza, Tent Rocks is a stunning natural stone gallery of cones and spires, serpentine canyons and striped mesas. On a nice day, it makes an ideal day-trip destination and offers one of the nicest short hikes in the state.

The story began a million years ago when volcanoes in the Jemez mountains exploded spewing rock and ash over hundreds of square miles, leaving a layer of volcanic debris 400 feet thick. The explosion blew out fifty cubic miles of dirt with a force of nearly 100 times that released at Mount St. Helens. The hot particles fused together forming a firm yet porous rock known as tuff — an amalgam of volcanic ash, pumice, irregular rock fragments and bits of obsidian known as Apache tears.

For centuries, water running off the mountains cut into these soft deposits creating the narrow smooth-walled passages and the singular cone-shaped tent rock formations that stand along the edge of Canada Camada like pieces on a giant game board. Amazingly uniform in shape, the tent-like formations vary in height, some as tall as ninety feet.

Early hunter-gatherers may have been the first to see this area as it now is, leaving behind the petroglyphs pecked into the canyon walls. Excavations near Tent Rocks have unearthed fire pits and artifacts thought to be 5,000 years old.

The route to Tent Rocks leaves Interstate 25 at exit 264 to State Road 16, then right on State Road 22 then left on Tribal Road 92 to the Tent Rocks turnoff just before entering Cochiti Pueblo. From this last turn, it is three miles to the parking area where there is an information board, a restroom and several shaded picnic tables.

The trail begins at the information board and quickly enters a wide sandy wash bordered and shaded by ponderosa pines. Across the basin to the west, the base of the cliff is crowded with cones, their tops whipped into points like so many sandy, tan meringues.

The wash narrows steadily and funnels into a deep slit-like canyon, 400 hundred yards long and in places barely wide enough for two to pass. The walls of the serpentine canyon, sometimes rising 200 feet, have been scoured and smoothed by the rasp-like action of the silt-laden runoff. Embedded within the welded tuff, bits of obsidian glitter like black diamonds. Here and there, a lone and gnarled ponderosa clings valiantly to its niche high on the canyon wall. Cones and hoodoos like sculpted sentinels, stand guard at every turn.

At several places, the winding stone corridor has been partially blocked by huge fallen rocks, which have to be climbed over or, in one case, stooped under. Watch along the left for a small alcove where a tall ponderosa and a lone tent rock mark the site of petroglyphs — serpents, handprints and geometric shapes — carved into the cliff face.

Turning to the left, the canyon opens into a small amphitheatre bunched with red-barked manzanita bushes, before narrowing again to a rock-choked passage. Those who don't choose to turn around here scramble up through this passage and across a ridge to the mesa top, a great spot for a picnic and a panoramic view that includes the Rio Grande basin and the broad sweep of the Sangre de Cristos.

On the return trip, take the well-marked Cave Loop Trail, a scenic one-mile path that skirts around the base of the cliffs that form the walls of the basin. Along the way, you will pass a cave once used as a sheltered lookout by cowboys watching their stock — and probably by earlier watchers before them. The path back to the parking lot passes close to a number of the large tent-like cones. Along the way, keep an eye out for the tracks of coyotes, deer, elk and cougars that inhabit the area.

IF YOU GO . . .

A trip to Tent Rocks is a trip back in time. Here on display is the technicolor wreckage of a terrible geologic storm, sculpted by the relentless erosion of a million years of wind and water. It's a special place. It's a silent place. It's a place you will want to see again.

> ## IF YOU GO . . .
>
> The easy round-trip hike covers about two miles. Allow two to three hours. Visitation hours in winter (November 1 — March 31) are 8:00 A.M. to 5:00 P.M. and in summer (April 1 to October 31) 7:00 A.M. to 6:00 P.M. Spring and fall are ideal. Avoid winter hikes if there has been a heavy snowfall, which can block the narrow canyon. In the summer, take plenty of water and do not go into the canyon if there is any possibility of a thunderstorm in the Jemez. Entry fee, payable onsite, is five dollars for a private vehicle.

Hawk Watch

THE BIG HAWK HUNG ON THE WIND like a brown, broad-winged kite, fifty yards out and a hundred feet below me, the sun highlighting the russet feathers in his tail. Slowly he picked his way through the wind currents and drifted off to the southeast as if he were floating on the surface of an invisible sea. It was the first time any of us had seen a hawk in flight up close. It was the first of thirty we would see that day.

We had come to Capilla Peak southeast of Albuquerque on the advice of a friend who had told us about watching these magnificent birds in flight. Every year in September and October, raptors from all over the United States begin their annual migration to South America, a round trip of nearly, 15,000 miles. Birds from the Cascades and Northern Rockies stream south down their mountain flyways surfing the thermals and the air currents generated by the elevated terrain.

Ornithologists and naturalists in New Mexico observed that these migrating birds often use a slot in the Manzano Mountains to move from one side of the mountain range to the other to pick up more favorable currents. It was here on the point of a rocky ridge at 10,000 feet overlooking that slot that we had gathered to watch this remarkable ritual.

To reach the monitoring site we drove forty miles south from Albuquerque and took Forest Road 259 into the mountains. A short walk through the woods brought us to a bare rocky precipice protruding out into space. To the west and two thousand feet below us, the Rio Grande valley stretched away into the pastels of the distance

If You Go . . .

like a tight, tan drumhead trimmed only by the green braid of cottonwoods along the river.

Our instructor was a pleasant young man from Hawk Watch International, a non-profit membership organization staffed mainly by volunteers. Hawk Watch promotes conservation of raptors — eagles, hawks and other birds of prey — characterized by sharp clutching talons, superior eyesight and hooked beaks capable of tearing meat.

The focal point of their research is long-term, largescale monitoring of raptor populations along their migration flyways in western North America. By using a standardized method of counting — at some sites for more than fifteen consecutive years — Hawk Watch has accumulated a data base that has become an important source of information for understanding the status and trends of western raptor populations.

Of unquestionable aesthetic value, raptors also represent an important link in the food chain of life. They are efficient predators and keep populations of their prey — insects, small mammals, passerine birds (perching and songbirds) — in balance with their own food supply. In addition, raptors often prey on the infirm and disabled animals in a population, helping to eliminate disease and, by insuring a healthy gene pool, helping to insure the survival of the fittest.

As predators feeding at the top of the food chain, gathering food from widely dispersed sources, raptors are vulnerable to environmental disruption and contamination and can serve as excellent barometers of ecosystem problems. Thirty years ago, studies showed that a decline in the raptor populations led to the first concerns about the hazards of the pesticide DDT.

Hawk Watch currently conducts migration counts along ten strategic flyways in seven western states. In addition to two sites in New Mexico, there are monitoring stations in Nevada, Utah, Arizona, Montana, Oregon and Washington.

The largest monitoring site is in eastern Mexico on the coastal plain of Veracruz where, during the peak of the fall migration season, hundreds of thousands of raptors can be seen each day as they travel south to Central and South America for the winter.

On our day at the Manzano site, the primary interest was the hawk migration. The hawk family includes accipiters and buteos. Accipters are long-tailed hawks with short, rounded wings, ideal for navigating the woodland habitat where they feed on smaller birds. The most common western accipiters are the Cooper's hawk and the sharp-shinned hawk. Buteos are large hawks, such as the red-tailed hawk, with broad wings and wide, rounded tails, built for sustained soaring in high, wide circles.

Since 1985, members of Hawk Watch have gathered at the Manzano site to count and identify these birds as they migrate south. Part of the monitoring program here and at other sites involves trapping and banding a sample of the migrating birds to learn more about the health and condition of the raptor population. The recovery of previously banded hawks adds critical information about their migratory habits and natural longevity.

To trap the birds, blinds constructed of hay bales and sticks are built on rocky outcroppings along the birds' line of flight. A pigeon, tethered by one leg, is staked out in front of the blind. When a hawk makes a pass at the pigeon, spring-loaded nets are fired into the air, trapping the bird. The nets are constructed such that the birds are not injured by the trapping, even the peregrine falcons that come into the trap nets at speeds approaching 180 miles per hour. The decoy trapping system is so effective that one falcon was caught five times on the same day.

The captured birds are carefully examined to determine their age and physical condition. Various measurements are made and leg bands are placed. The birds are then brought up to the rocky observation point for release.

Our instructor gently removed the bird from the metal tube in which he had been placed to calm him. It was a male red-tailed hawk, three years old and in good condition. When the time came to release our bird, the instructor held his gloved hand aloft and gave the bird a soft toss. With three hard flaps of its wings it climbed into the wind and banked off to the south.

If You Go . . .

Hawk Watch estimates that they see about forty percent of the birds that migrate past the Manzano station. On a typical day there are about 150 to 200 sightings and ten to fifteen birds are banded. An average of 4,000 migrating raptors are recorded here each season.

Not all the birds survive the long migration. Some of the birds are killed by humans, or natural predators. Others, the less skilled hunters, die of starvation. Estimates are difficult because only about 1 percent of the banded birds are recovered, but the mortality for juveniles making their first trek may be as high as fifty percent.

As the day passed I learned to identify the birds, sometimes spotting them before other members of the group. I could pick out the broad, square wings and blunt tails of the butoes and the long, straight tails of the accipiters — the Cooper's hawks and the sharp shins, their wings flexed gull-like and shoulders hunched slightly as if they were cold.

While we ate lunch, Clark's nutcrackers played in the pines. A squadron of Cooper's hawks cruised by on their way over to the eastern slope. Later a flight of tiny swifts suddenly came sailing up over the ridge top like feathered shrapnel blown up out of the canyon.

At four o'clock the instructor brought up the last bird for release, a female sharp shin. She sat for a moment on the instructor's hand, her hooded eyes studying us. Then, with a quick flap she was airborne, sailing out over the wooded slopes, out over the tan valley. She hung in the air for a moment over the horizon and the cement skyline of the city twenty miles away then, dipping a wing, banked off down the wind out of sight and back into the wild.

If you go . . .

Hawk migration counts are coordinated by Hawk Watch International and are conducted in New Mexico every year in the Manzano Mountains (September 10 — October 20) and the Sandia Mountains (March 10 — May 10). Hawk Watch provides educational programs with slide shows and live birds for interested schools and organizations

For more information, write to Hawk Watch International, Inc., P.O. Box 660, Salt Lake City, Utah, 84110-0660 or call 800-726-HAWK or see their Web site at www.infoxpress.com.hawkwatch.

Utah's Canyon Country By RV

GO AHEAD. LAUGH AT THOSE OLD GEEZERS in their boxy aluminum RVs. It might be hard for them to find a parking place in Palm Beach, but out in southern Utah's painted high lonesome, where motels are scarcer than discouraging words, it's the only way to travel.

Every year, agencies rent RVs to more than 35,000 people and rentals are increasing by thirty percent a year. RV enthusiasts choose this style of travel because it provides a combination of explorer's freedom and armchair convenience unmatched by any other form of travel. The versatile self-sufficiency of these campers allows access to areas too remote for easy auto travel without the tyranny of a tour bus. It's a style of travel whose time has come.

So when it came time for our Utah trip, I recalled the wanderlust that always came over me when I passed one of these schooners on the highway. We rented a twenty-four-footer, small enough for a novice to handle and large enough so the bed didn't have to be converted to a dining room table each day — an exercise that complicates the morning routine.

And we were away — New Age explorers sailing down the south wind in our chrome-plated cruiser, bound for the slickrock and canyon country and ten days of wilderness peace and quiet. A walk-through tour and video had familiarized us with the features of our motor home, including the operation of the furnace and the air conditioner, water supply, sewage disposal system and the refrigerator. (doesn't operate if the RV is not level).

The first day we drove 300 easy miles through the mountainous pine cover of northern New Mexico to our destination in the foothills of the Rockies, an RV park that we had chosen from the guide book given to us by the rental agency. Driving the twenty-four-foot unit with automatic transmission was easier than we expected, and we cruised along smoothly at highway speeds.

Each of the RV park's campsites was thoughtfully spaced in a stand of ponderosa pines and was equipped with a well for fresh water and an outlet for electricity. Use of these "hook-ups" was optional. We didn't use them since our RV battery would provide lights for twelve hours (it is recharged daily during the drive) and our freshwater tank held fifty gallons — about enough, we discovered, for two days including hot showers.

We positioned our camper with a sunset view from our dinner table and built a fire in the fire pit with wood that we had brought along in one of the unit's large compartments. While the fire burned down to steak-cooking coals, we had a glass of wine and watched the slow motion of a perfect sunset, soothed by the silence and the perfume of pine needles. You can't get that at your average Doubletree Inn.

Morning began at sunup with the first rays streaming through the window of our cozy bedroom. We decided to have breakfast inside, and while the coffee was brewing, we showered and dressed. Some mornings when it was cool, we took our coffee back to bed and enjoyed the view while the RV was warmed by the furnace. This is camping with climate control. Everyday a room and a restaurant with a view.

By 9:30 a.m we were off, headed west under an achey-breaky-heart blue sky into Red Rock country —the land of Butch Cassidy and complementary colors. The temperature rose with the mounting sun and dried the land as we approached. The cool colors of the mountains yielded to the earth tones of the high desert. The ponderosa pines were replaced by widely spaced junipers and piñons standing on the edge of their blue shadows. Networks of dry streambeds and arroyos with eroded, fluted walls etched the sandy land, leaving it as tanned and finely worked as a hand-tooled saddle.

If You Go . . .

Pink sandstone bluffs, like great flushed cheeks, rose up as if annoyed out of the space around us. As we drove along in air-conditioned comfort, we were bathed in the stereo sounds of Maria Callas, perhaps the one voice with the power and range to provide a soundtrack for this vast and varied land.

At noon we picnicked in a streamside cottonwood grove at Newspaper Rock. Here, under a protective rock overhang, hundreds of figures, some more than 4,000 years old, have been pecked into the dark patina of the desert varnish by early American Indians, for whatever reason, bored or awed.

North of Moab is the wind-chiseled wonderland of Arches National park — 114 square miles of salmon-colored sandstone wind-carved into an amazing array of bold towers, pinnacles and spires and some 2,000 arches, one spanning more than 300 feet from base to base. We parked near the cinnamon remnants of a log cabin and began the two-hour climb to Delicate Arch. The trail wound up through the silence, over slick rock marked with cairns, through narrow draws and along a ledge to a perfect amphitheater where, its bowed legs framing the La Sal Mountains, the arch-of-them-all teetered on the edge of a sandstone bowl.

We lingered, at once startled and soothed, awed by the space and drawn to the detail, watching the play of light on the rocks. Nearly a roll of film later we headed back, our minds and our cameras filled with images of color, form and grace.

We drove back through the park, through miles of now-shadowed grandeur, under great sheer cathedral-like cliffs, between standing rock fins and balanced rocks, past windowed arches, bridges and spires and monoliths with names like Park Avenue, Court House Rock and Parade of the Elephants.

Just before sunset we arrived at our campsite on Dead Horse Point, a peninsula of elevated land jutting out into the space and rock wildness of Canyonlands National Park's 600 square miles. From the point the land falls away in scoured and terraced multicolored cliffs to the floor of the canyon cut by the Colorado and Green Rivers. Here it's easy to see that, more than anything else, the West is the work of water. The water is gone now, but like a hit-and-run driver, it did its damage and disappeared, leaving behind a million square miles of wrinkled fenders and scraped paint.

As we stood watching the canyons fill with shadow, there was not one sign of man and not one sound except the echoed cries of the ravens as they blew by calling each other names. Unable to give up on the night, we sat by the warmth and woody incense of our piñon fire and talked under a black sky shot full of bright holes. Yes, Virginia, there is a Milky Way.

In the morning, we drove back toward Moab, descending along Sevenmile Canyon through a wonderland of rock formations. Die-cut buttes and mesas, their cliffs being reduced to rusty rubble, squared off the skyline. Towering bluffs of Wingate sandstone, as smooth as blocks of brown ice, crowded the road into the narrow canyon.

South of Moab we found the Slickrock Trail and climbed with it over twenty miles of rolling Navajo sandstone mounds, petrified dunes, crotched with tamarisk and cottonwood and perfectly bleached datura, then descended through the spires and towers of Castle Valley to the Colorado River canyon.

We crossed the river and the canyon north of Moab to Potash Road, one of the most scenic drives in the country. For fifteen miles this well-engineered road follows the Colorado River where there are turnouts for viewing a prehistoric granary, dinosaur tracks and several panels of well-preserved petroglyphs attributed to the vanished Fremont Indians who roamed this canyon land 1,000 years ago.

The next day we were off to Capitol Reef, one of the nations most exotic but least known national parks. Capitol Reef lies ninety miles due west of Dead Horse Point across the impenetrable Canyonlands Maze. To reach it requires a three-hour drive, looping north to I-70, then south to Utah Highway 24 through some of the most strikingly desolate landscape to be reached by car.

Here is the bedrock of the continent stripped of its party clothes. To the east, fifty miles of poor sand hills stretch out into a thin, tight line with nothing but clouds to cast a shadow. To the west, the escarpment of the San Rafael Reef lies along the horizon for thirty

If You Go . . .

miles like a serrated dike, striped with the purple and gray of the fifty-million-year-old Morrison formation.

We passed through the lunar landscape of Caineville and Hanksville, under the shadow of the 12,000-foot Henry Mountains, the last area surveyed in the continental United States, then turned west along the Fremont River flowing like liquid adobe, first between great pleated slopes of dark Mancos shale, then between cliffs topped with capitol-like domes of white Navajo sandstone.

Set aside as a national monument in 1937, Capitol Reef's geologic wonders were so isolated and remote that it was not until 1971 that it received National Park status. There is still an atmosphere of remoteness and solitude not found at other parks.

We signed in at the park campground, a peaceful oasis along the Fremont River, shaded by ancient cottonwoods — one with a girth of more than twenty feet — then headed south on Scenic Drive along the flanks of cliffs layered with bands of pink and purple and green and gray. We passed the many trailheads that led to the network of hiking trails that crisscross the area.

East of Fruita we found the tailhead to Hickman Bridge. If you have time for only one hike, take this moderate two-miler for a good look at the backcountry. It is testimony to the secrecy of this eroded, broken country that this magnificent natural bridge was rediscovered in 1940 after remaining hidden for sixty-five years, though it is only two miles from the highway.

The trail crosses a boulder-strewn ridge clumped with chamisa and silver-green buffaloberry to a walled streambed carved into the sandstone. We followed the stream, now reduced to potholes and water pockets, past the stick-and-mud remains of a Fremont Indian granary to the last turning and the bridge.

This graceful span, fifteen feet thick at its center, arched 125 feet over us, bridging a gap 133 feet from base to base. Climbing behind the bridge we could see, through its arched space, the perfectly framed white mass of Capitol Dome.

Beyond Fruita to the west climbed to Gooseneck Point for a view of the 500-foot deep looping curves cut by Sulphur Creek into the tan Kaibab limestone, then, just before sunset, drove to Panorama Point for the most spectacular view in the park. To the south, the valley sweeps out of sight along the technicolor bulk of the Waterpocket Fold. Directly across and reddened by the setting sun, stands one of the most striking land forms in the West — the pillared and fanned pipe-organ façade of Castle Butte.

Perhaps the most scenic drive in Utah's canyon country is the 100-mile trip from Capitol Reef to Bryce Canyon along Utah Highway 12. It begins by ascending through the pine and aspen forests of 11,600-foot Boulder Mountain, one of America's highest plateaus, to the town of Boulder, which, until 1939, received its mail by pack mule. Here we stopped at the Anasazi Indian Village Historical Monument, where we browsed through an excellent visitor's center and eighty-seven excavated rooms of an 1100 A.D. Anasazi village.

From Boulder, the Escalante Grand Staircase, recently designated as a national monument, begins its spectacular descent through some of the most remote country in the United States. Sloping down through layer after layer of handsomely sculptured sandstone, the road enters the suddenly lush Calf Creek Canyon. Unhurried, we decided on another diversion and pulled into the nearly empty parking area.

We packed a picnic and headed into the narrow box canyon which early stockmen found ideal for corralling their calves. The path led through meadows filled with Indian paintbrush, aster, primrose and gilia, then between biscuit-colored sandstone cliffs which soon forced the track along the stream, gurgling over gravel beds and beaver dams where trout sunned in the clear water.

We stopped for lunch in a shaded glen and, as we ate, studied the 1,000 year-old petroglyphs and storage huts niched in the canyon walls. Another hour along we came to the end of the canyon at Lower Calf Creek Falls, where the stream cascades through 126 feet of hanging garden into a deep pool — a scene more like Hawaii than the High Southwest.

From Calf Creek the road climbed the forested flank of 8,000-foot Paunsaugunt Plateau to our campground in the woods, easy walking distance from the rim of Bryce Canyon. After a visit to the

If You Go . . .

informative visitor's center — a mandatory stop — we walked to one of the many overlooks. The view was as breathtaking as advertised.

There, spread out before us, was ten square miles of stone fairyland. Thousands of tightly packed and multicolored stone totems, striped and stacked and inflamed by the setting sun, poked up from the basin floor. The scene resembled a city of great pillared and painted temples with all their roofs blown away. Hypnotized by the play of light on the multicolored columns, we stayed until darkness drove us to our fireside, still amazed.

The next morning we hiked down Navajo Loop into the canyon's stony maze. For hours we wandered the intricate passageways, crowded between skyscraper-sized rock towers, sometimes so close that only patches of sky showed above us. From the cracked canyon floor, huge Douglas firs rose 100 feet toward the light. It was indeed, as settler Ebenezer Bryce had said, "a 'helluva' place to lose a cow."

The path wound along dry stream beds, through the cool caverns of Wall Street, past galleries of formations with names like The Gossips, The Organ Grinder's Monkey and the Wise Men — forms which led the early Piute Indians to describe the basin as the "place of red rock standing like men in a bowl-shaped canyon."

More over-awed than finished, we climbed back to the rim and picnicked under the shade of a 1,000 —year old bristle cone pine looking out over the canyon across the pastels of southern Utah to the profile of Navajo Mountain ninety miles away. We would leave behind for another trip more than sixty miles of trails to secret hollows, caves and canyons.

The next day we drove south on Utah's Bicentennial Highway 90. In spite of its rocky bravado, this is a fragile land. Along the lee of the Henry Mountains evidence of erosion is everywhere apparent. Talus slopes, like piles of broken pastel chalk, lie at the base of every cliff, perfectly angled as if drawn with a protractor. Deep fissures scar the slopes. The flats are littered with the outwash rubble left by the vanished waters.

We stopped for a picnic on a red bluff overlooking the north end of 186-mile-long Lake Powell. There was so little traffic that drivers stopped in the road to take photographs. Five hundred feet below us, sunlight ricocheted off the waters of the Colorado River, here tamed in its journey through country so remote that it passes only three towns along its 1,000-mile course from Moab, Utah to Needles, California.

Already charting our next trip, we tacked toward home across a vast grassland sea under a pure and seamless sky, our only landmark the blue bulk of Sleeping Ute Mountain on the horizon. As we topped one last swell back into New Mexico, with the strains of Maria's cadenzas ringing in our ears, the dark form of Shiprock, under full sail, hove into view.

If you go...

▲ The Recreational Vehicle Rental Association offers a thirty-eight-page directory of more than 270 rental companies. A copy can be obtained by sending ten dollars to RVRA, 3030 University Drive, Fairfax, VA 22030-2515.

▲ Woodall's Campground Directory (Western Edition) is an inclusive guide to campsites in the southwest and is available for $12.95 by calling 800-323-9076. Use the book to call ahead for reservations at the next day's destination. Otherwise, plan to stop by 2:00 P.M.

▲ State campgrounds often offer the best combination of cost, ambiance and privacy. Commercial sites offer the most amenities (stores, washer/dryer, restaurants) but are usually more crowded. Most campsites will allow you to fill your water tank and dump waste for a small fee even if you are not staying there. Firewood is often scarce. Bring your own or buy bundles at the campgrounds.

A Costa Rican Tour At A Leisurely Pace

I WAITED IN THE DARKNESS on a makeshift ferry landing forty miles from Costa Rica's border with Panama. Overhead, the skeletal steel latticework of an unfinished bridge across the Rio Grande de Terraba was just visible against the night sky. Watching the primitive ferry's single running light move slowly across the dark water, I was struck by the fact that, in this high-tech era, the road connecting the continents of North and South America is bridged by such a fragile link.

My wife and I had come to Costa Rica on a week-long trip in January to see the rain forest. But long before we boarded the ferry to the forest preserve, we had discovered several other natural wonders in this country of jungle and coastal plains, deserted beaches and fertile valleys, and a range of mountains so high that it is possible to see from their peaks both the Atlantic and the Pacific oceans.

We had arrived in San Jose on the night flight from Miami. As we approached the coastline from the Caribbean, the jungle was black below us except for the lights of the three main cities of the Central Valley — San Jose, Heredia and Cartago.

Within an hour we had rented a car and were navigating San Jose's intricate civic gridwork. On a quiet side street near Parque Bolivar, we found Hotel L'Ambiance looking reassuringly like its brochure, a white one-story stucco building with a red tile roof, well lighted and welcoming. Guest rooms with names like Buena Vida and Tranquillidad opened directly onto the patio. In the center of the patio, a white cockatoo napped in a bamboo cage next to a tiered fountain surrounded by pots of pink azaleas.

Inside, Buena Vida was spacious and tropical, with tall shuttered windows, dark woodwork and antique Victorian furniture. A mahogany fan, suspended over the bed from the twelve-foot ceiling, turned slowly. In the soft darkness, the quiet was broken only by the dripping of the fountain and the occasional complaints of the cockatoo.

Breakfast was served in the patio, and, as we ate we began to adjust to the largo rhythm of the tropics. It was ten o'clock before we left, bound for the rain forests of Coto Brus.

Travel south from San Jose is along one of two routes. We selected the coastal route, which first goes west along the old Spanish road to Orotina, then south. Our return would be through the Valle del General and over the 11,000-foot Cordillera de Talamanca. The drive, a 400-mile circuit, proved ideal for the first-time visitor, ensuring a thorough sample of the country's varied topography.

Barely the size of West Virginia, Costa Rica is squeezed into the only available space between two oceans and two continents. But the distances are deceptive, and like many other things about Costa Rica, have no relation to time. The roads are often rough and dusty, sometimes with terrible and unexpected potholes, and the high heat and humidity encourage slow motion and deliberation.

About twenty-five miles from San Jose, we crossed a northern spur of the Talamanca Mountains through broken jungle hills brightened by the yellow tops of flowering cortesa amarilla trees and the shiny green plots of coffee planted on slopes that seemed too steep to harvest. Here we encountered the first of the "living fences" we would see all week. Tree limbs, often dracena, stuck into the ground for fence posts, take root and thrive in the fertile volcanic soil.

Near Jaco, one of Costa Rica's many beach towns, we stopped at a café by the sea. Swimmers and surfers crossed the road to small hotels and restaurants concealed in the trees. Cooled by the shade and the ocean breeze, we drank aqua dulce — a drink of sweetened water — while frigate birds hung in the sky like black kites and squadrons of pelicans patrolled the bright beaches. At a fruit stand, for two dollars, we bought pineapples, papayas and mangoes, which we would have for breakfast for the next two days. We ate the zapote —

If You Go . . .

which resembles a sweet avocado with orange pulp — for lunch, sectioning the firm orange fruit and eating it as we drove.

At Parrita, about ninety miles from San Jose, the paved road ended and the palms began marking the first of the plantations that extended along the coastal road for nearly eighty miles. Planted to replace the aging banana plantations and harvested for oil, these uniform palms — all about thirty feet tall — back away from the road in dark rows toward the hills a mile away, their neat ranks broken only by the rectangular settlements for the plantation workers built along the road at five-mile intervals. Resembling military posts, these compounds have six or eight wooden and screened buildings arranged around three sides of a clipped soccer field, their faded pastels contrasting with the scarlet brilliance of the hibiscus hedges.

Just outside Quepos, we waited while a tour bus squeezed across the narrow bridge made of wooden rails laid crosswise on a wooden frame. Once a busy banana port, the laid-back town is now gateway to Manuel Antonio Park, one of Costa Rica's thirty national wilderness preserves.

The village's single paved street is a palm-lined boulevard, bordered on one side by a row of pastel buildings and plastered cantinas, and on the other by a beach and a broad estuary where shacks on stilts stand in the water beside their reflections like wooden herons.

We found Villas Nicolas, out first day's destination, in the hills behind the town. Shaded by banana trees, this charming Mediterranean-style villa is a series of connected white stucco apartments stacked down the face of the hill, each with Spartan furnishings and its own covered balcony to ensure privacy and an unobstructed view of the sea.

From the hammock on the balcony, we could see birds and butterflies in the trees just out of reach. Then it was off to the open-air restaurant for a dinner of rolled corvina (sea bass) with sautéed onions and Creole sauce, cups of rich Costa Rican coffee, and the first of what was to be a week-long series of superb coconut flans.

The next morning I was awakened by the rhythmic hiss of the surf through the open window, and the sound of monkeys bickering in the trees just down the hill. At breakfast, black birds with rumps the color of hibiscus blossoms flitted in the trees and capuchin monkeys watched us through palm fronds they parted with their hands like Venetian blinds.

At nearby Manuel Antonio Park, Espadilla, the first of three beaches, is a mile long scimitar of white sand, curved slightly and backed by sea grape and coconut palms. Behind the beach, the jungle foliage is thick and unbroken except for a few clearings for small hotels and cottages. We found a place in the shade under the sea grape trees and spent the afternoon swimming and reading and watching brown boys playing in the surf.

Late in the day, we walked to the end of the untracked beach and waded across a small estuary into the main part of the park, where there are two more beaches, smaller and more sheltered, each a perfect white crescent. We joined a group on a park trail just in time to see the tour guide pointing out a three-toed sloth lounging in a cercopia tree where it spends its entire life in symbiotic partnership with colonies of venomous ants. The ants discourage the jungle cats that might otherwise find the sloth easy prey.

We sat for a while watching a family of white-faced monkeys, some with babies on their backs, as they played in the trees, alternately performing and watching for our approval. As we returned along the beach path just before dark, a coatimundi, as if on some appointed errand, walked casually out of the jungle and crossed the path just ahead of us.

The next morning we headed through twenty miles of palm plantations to Dominical. Just south of the little town, on a high point of land by the sea, we stopped for lunch at Cabinas Punta Dominical. In this little small compound are four rustic cabins built of tropical hardwood and a delightful, cliff-top restaurant, thatch-roofed against the rain, but open on all sides to allow views of the ocean and the thirty miles of crescent beach curving into the blued distance of the Peninsula de Osa. Punta Dominical would be the perfect place to disappear from the world, a place to write a book or wait for a romantic rendezvous.

If You Go . . .

From Domical, we crossed the mountains to San Isidro in the Valle de General, then picked up the Inter-American Highway and followed it south in the gathering dusk through miles of gently rolling pineapple plantations toward San Vito and the coffee hills of Coto Brus.

A wrong turn at Paseo Real used up the last of the daylight, and after a roadside conference with two helpful truck drivers and another hour of driving, we found ourselves at the ferry crossing. Guided onto the primitive barge by the beam of a single flashlight, our car, another car and a van bumped aboard the little vessel, filling all the available space on the open deck, and rode over the dark water while the two boatmen worked silently in the darkness of the crossing.

Another hour on, four miles outside San Vito, we arrived at the Wilson Botanical garden and were met by Gail Hewson, my wife's sister, and Luis Diego Gomez, the director of the rain forest station. At dinner, we could hear a chainsaw echoing in the night from the nearby Gamboa forest, an old-growth forest. Las Cruses Biological Station, of which Wilson Botanical Garden is a part, is trying to acquire that land before it is destroyed by lumbering.

Las Cruses consists of 360 acres of wilderness rain forest preserve, owned by the Organization for Tropical Studies, a consortium of fifty-three universities and research institutions with headquarters at Duke University. Within the twenty-five cultivated acres of the garden, containing one of the most important collections of tropical and subtropical plants in Central America, there are more than 2,000 species of native plants, as well as exotics from all over the world. In addition to the abundant plant life, there are 317 species of birds, thirty-five species of bats, 3,000 types of moths and butterflies and a wide variety of reptiles and mammals.

The preserve can accommodate thirty-two visitors in nine dormitory-style bunkrooms and four cabins that have living areas. Six miles of gently graded self-guided trails wind in switchbacks over the palm-covered hillsides among huge bunches of aroids, ferns, bromeliads, heliconias, marantacae, lilies and brilliant ginger batons. Blue butterflies flit under the rain forest canopy and hummingbirds buzz among the hibiscus hedges.

A Costa Rican Tour At A Leisurely Pace

On our first day, we walked with Gail along an abandoned woods road to the Rio Jaba, through a shaded corridor of greens, a hanging garden matted with moss, twining roots for steps. We passed a dozen or so people that day, some scientists and some tourists. Here grew hundreds of exotic and near-extinct plants and above them, trees of every shape and size woven into a two-tiered canopy that filtered out all but a sort of warm twilight.

The jungle, too thick to walk through, was tightly packed with ferns, veils of vines, primitive cycads — part fern, part palm — philodendron, croton, bamboo and towering gray cylinders of strangler figs with room enough inside for two people to stand. Quilts of impatiens — purple, rose, pink, salmon — grew on the ground under dracena and schefflera trees large enough for lumber. In the evening, we returned to the station for dinner on the balcony overlooking the garden and the woody broccoli of the rain forest.

For the return trip to San Jose, we took the highland road, along the mountains that lay down the center of the country like the spine of a great, green dragon. We stopped at San Vito long enough to stock up on coffee at two dollars a pound then drove back through the hills to the ferry crossing at Rio de Terraba. In the daylight it was much less foreboding that it had been the night of our arrival. At the steep landing, cars and trucks lined up on the dirt road and natives in colorful clothes sold cool drinks from the shade of their crude kiosks.

North of San Isidro, the road wound to the sky through rising hills, green and tangled with vegetation. Tiny orange orchids and calla lilies grew in the roadside ditches. As the altitude rose toward the summit at nearly 11,000 feet, the trees became progressively smaller and stunted until at the Cerro de la Muerte — the ridge of death — they gave way to buckbrush and thrifty, low tundra.

Often in the afternoon, the summit is shrouded in fog, but the day we crossed, it was clear enough to see, by just turning my head, the blue sweep of both the Atlantic and Pacific oceans. Standing there in the sunshine, it was hard to imagine the storms and frigid nighttime temperatures that had killed so many travelers trying to cross this high pass.

If you go . . .

▲ Information on Costa Rica is available from the Costa Rica Tourist board, P.O. Box 777, 10000 San Jose, Costa Rica, 880-343-6332. Several air carriers including United, American, Continental and Lacasa offer flights to Costa Rica. Rental cars are available at Juan Santamaria International Airport in San Jose from Hertz, Avis, National and Budget.

▲ The average annual rainfall at Las Cruses is 157 inches coming mostly from September to November. The driest months are December and April. The temperature is determined more by the altitude than the season with daily averages of 71 to 92 degrees along the coast and 61 to 77 degrees at higher elevations.

Where to Stay
▲ **Hotel L'Ambiance** has seven rooms with private baths 506-222-6702.
▲ **Villas Nicolas** 506-777-0481.
▲ **Wilson Botanical Garden** 506-773-3278.

Springtime In Provence

BRACED AGAINST AN UNEXPECTED CHILL, we huddled in the pre-dawn darkness beneath the ruined ramparts of Les Baux Castle. Overhead, ravens blew by calling each other names, struggling against the mistral that had swept in during the night and threatened to blow us, too, from our perch.

We had climbed to the keep of the most imposing medieval castle ruin in Provence to watch the Easter sunrise. The cliff-top citadel, hewn from and part of the great white rock ridge on which it sits, was home to the iron-fisted seigneurs of Les Baux, one of the most feared and powerful families of feudal France. From our vantage point among the wind-swept rubble, a patterned landscape of olive groves and vineyards sloped away from the cliff base to the limestone backbone of the Alpilles Range five miles away. Under the overcast sky, we waited for the sunrise that never came. It wasn't the weather we had expected in Provence in April, but it was our only bad day.

My wife and I had come to Provence in the spring, a perfect time to see this sensuous country of Roman ruins, Rhone wine and ratatouille at its seductive best. The gardens are filled with flowers, the nighttime temperatures are warm enough to dine out and the roads are not yet crowded with tourists and travel trailers. We arranged to travel by car to get a better feel for the country, using a small hostellerie as a home base for day-trips to the vineyards, the medieval hill towns and the coast.

We landed in Paris and by midmorning were aboard a silver and orange train to Avignon gliding along at speeds in excess of 100 miles

If You Go . . .

per hour. As we sped south under the heightening sky, we passed from the worn pastels of Paris to the primary colors of Provence. The tile roofs grew redder, bright poppies bloomed in the roadside ditches, and the field crops of rapeseed, as yellow as saffron, alternated with clean-cut rectangles of plowed black dirt. Over the warming land, cumulus clouds bloomed in a sky the color of enameled Creuset cookware.

We picked up our rental car in Avignon and after a thirty minute drive, we arrived at the charming stone simplicity of our hotel for the week — le Mas d' Aigret. Built in the 1630s, in the shadow of the crags of Les Baux castle, the old farmhouse was converted into a hotel seventy-five years ago and is now run by a retired English journalist and his French wife.

The two-story limestone building, with red roof tiles and shutters the color of wisteria, has sixteen bedrooms, each with a private balcony or garden shaded by olive and pine trees and surrounded by flowering plants and decorative terraced retaining walls.

The food alone would be reason enough to select this charming hostellerie and, indeed, half the dinner guests each evening were either locals or guests of other hotels in the area. The restaurant is carved from the rocks under the hotel and was the original cave of the old farmhouse. The violet stain of wine fumes is still visible on the quarried ceiling.

For our first dinner there was crepinee of quail and lentils in balsamic vinegar and roast lamb in garlic créme and a citron tart with dark chocolate sauce that was so good I was unable to resist it for three nights straight.

The next morning, after a sunny breakfast in our garden, we began our compass-point tour by first heading east to the Coulon Valley and the hill towns of the Luberon. As we left Les Baux, we drove through the olive groves at Mausanne, home of France's finest olive oil, where sun-browned men pruning the trees burned the cuttings at smoky fires. We passed dormant vineyards, with their winter winestock pruned and still bare, cemetery-like, standing row on row like hundreds of knobby brown crosses. The roads, even the secondary ones, were in excellent condition and the traffic surprisingly light.

Beyond Cavillon, we entered the valley of the medieval hill towns, fortified villages built in the thirteenth century. Set at intervals of ten to fifteen miles, these conical stone towns, the color of madeleins, spiral upward along their curved ramparts to the pinnacle of a castle ruin, rising above the valley floor like pointed pieces on a game board.

Our first stop, Oppede-le-Vieux, the most austere and imposing of all the hilltop villages, sits piled on a rocky spur halfway up the north slope of the Petit Luberon. The village is built of gray stone blocks that appear, from a distance, to have tumbled down the face of the hill from the ruined chateau above.

Deserted except for a few summer residents, Oppede has one small seasonal hotel and two open-air cafes. Otherwise, the only sign of life was the wisp of smoke at a chimney, potted flowers on a stone stoop or lace curtains in a dark window.

Meeting few other tourists, we climbed the narrow cobbled streets of the village, through the arches and the winding masonry canyons to the shell of the chateau that stood like a war ruin at the top of the hill. In the quiet damp of the close passages, it was nearly possible to hear the clank of armor and the clatter of horses' hooves on the stony way.

From Oppede, we drove through the tightly stacked, blond-stone geometry of Menerbes, then on to Bonnieux, the busiest and biggest of the hill towns. We stopped at the Café Cleric for coffee and its commanding view of the Luberon and then looked in at the cozy Hostellerie du Prieure, runner-up in our research for the perfect Provencal hotel. In the afternoon, we picnicked on pate, crusty bread, cornichons and a refreshing Tavel rose in the shadow of Lacoste, the gloomy stronghold of the Marquis de Sade.

Bypassing trendy Gordes, we drove northeast across the valley to Rousillon, the most photogenic of the hill towns. Perched on a spectacular hilltop site, the russet and mauve buildings of this stone village reflect the colors of the surrounding cliffs, stained — so the story goes — by the blood of a woman who threw herself to her

If You Go . . .

death after learning that she had eaten a stew made from the body of her murdered lover.

Nearly a roll of film later, we drove on, our minds and our cameras filled with images of terracotta facades, of bold blue doors and shutters of turquoise and dark green, of square mauve clock towers and step stone stairways, of shadowy arches and tiny pink squares crowded with bright red enameled chairs. The next day we headed south.

Not many Americans get to Cassis. Drawn to the more well known meccas of the Riviera, they miss this little gem of a sea town fifty miles south of Aix. Cassis is as colorful as a carnival. Wedged tightly into a rocky niche between the cliffs and the sea, the yellow and rose and white buildings of this little plaster town, red-roofed and brightly shuttered, are stacked down the hill in a pastel arc against the sea. At the foot of town, the slit of a harbor is filled with painted wooden boats and water the color of blue gin.

We wandered the morning streets, shopping for lavender and postcards, then sat in the perfect temperature of the park where men in shirtsleeves played and argued at boules on sand courts under the plane trees. Along the stone quay, couples with cameras and colorful clothes browsed under the awnings at waterfront shops or drank coffee at cafes with umbrella-shaded tables. Babies slept in carriages. Children licked fruit ices. Red, white and blue flags snapped in the wind.

For lunch there was bouride with aioli and piled plates of garlicky, stuffed mussels and fresh bread and a quenching white Cassis wine. We bought ice cream and walked to the beach at the end of the quay where we spent the rest of the afternoon under the cerulean sky watching the day wear itself out against the sea.

North of Les Baux, just beyond Avignon on the bank of the Rhone, are the vineyards of Chateauneuf-du-Pape which produce, with the possible exception of the roses of Tavel, the best-known wines of Provence. Here the vines are mulched with river stones that hold the heat of the sun after dark, increasing this muscular wine's alcohol content.

The day we visited Chateau Beaurenard, the parking lot at the well-kept, blue shuttered vineyard was empty. We spent an hour with the manager, sampling the vintages, then bought all the bottles we could carry. All survived the return trip to Les Baux except for one particularly fine '92 which we sampled, and then finished at a picnic later that afternoon near Venasque.

This little gray village, stacked on a rocky promontory, has one of the prime vistas in Provence. To the south, wooded hills rise to the ridges of the Petit Luberon. To the west, the Plateau de Vaucluse drops away to the Rhone. To the north, Mount Ventoux, its broad limestone top gleaming in the sun, lies across the horizon like a great white washed dike.

In the turnings of the empty streets lilacs grew behind garden walls and wisteria draped the gates. There was no sound except for our echoing steps and the lapping of water in the tiny fountained squares and, on the quarter hour, the measured blang of the thirteenth century church bell.

West of Les Baux is St. Remy, the gardening center of Provence. Plants and produce from this fertile plain are shipped all over France. The roads into this town from all directions are lined with greenhouses and narrow, cultivated fields partitioned by windbreaks of cypress trees that stab at the sky like rows of black daggers.

The town of St. Remy is a technicolor, sunlit charmer. The town center is ringed with wide streets, lined and roofed over with knobby plane trees and paved with their dappled shade. Under the trees, shoppers in colorful spring mufti mill about, stopping under the bright awnings to study the posted menus of the sidewalk cafes. Old men in black sweaters read newspapers in the square or sit in the sun around fountains filled by puff-faced cherubs spouting water.

Within the city's shaded circle, the streets are crowded with balconied apartments and tiny shops selling everything from antiques to artichokes to yard goods and yeast. At one wine shop, a five-liter jug of vin du pays sold for the equivalent of six dollars.

Just south of St. Remy are the excavated remains of Glanum, a Roman village. Its ruins, covered by silt washed down from the slopes of the Alpilles, were not exposed again until excavation began in 1920. Among the remarkable relics are the foundations of two grand homes, fountains, baths and temples. Across the road, like furniture forgotten

If You Go . . .

by the movers, stand Les Antiques — a triumphal arch that marked the end of the Roman road from Arles to Glanum, and a mausoleum, a memorial to Caesar and Augustus built in the first century A.D.

Nearby is St.-Paul-de-Mausole, the monastery where Van Gogh was confined in 1889 after cutting off his ear. It is possible to visit the cloister and walk the flowered grounds and, with the aid of guiding signs, stand where Van Gogh stood as he worked.

Our last evening found us in Mausanne, a one-street village three miles south of Les Baux, where we sat out the twilight at a small café drinking pastis with the locals and trying to translate a two-day old copy of *Le Monde*. We talked the bartender out of two of the short, thick pastis glasses which I now keep on a shelf behind the sink. Just a glance at those glasses, even on the coldest day, brings back the warmth of that April afternoon.

If you go . . .

▲ High-speed rail service leaves Paris for the four-hour trip to Avignon twice a day. Reservations are required and are available from Rail Europe, 800-848-7245.

▲ A car, required to see Provence, can be rented from the Hertz office near the station in Avignon. A valid U.S. driver's license is required

▲ The tourist season begins in late May and peaks in July and August. The weather in April is delightful, averaging 55 degrees at night and 70 degrees during the day.

▲ Americans will love the customer-oriented service at Mas d'Aigret. This, and other accommodations, can be found in the guide, Independent Chateau and Hotels, available from 15 rue Malebranche, 75005, Paris and from Hideaways Guide, 800-843-4433.

For Rent: Your Own House In The Tuscan Hills
Comfort, Cucina and Rooms with a View

FORGET FLORENCE. RESCHEDULE THAT TRIP TO ROME. Quit thinking of Italy as a museum. This year, head for the pastoral peace and quiet of the sunlit Tuscan hills, and what better way to see this land of Chianti, crostini and castellos than from the private comfort of your own rented house. It's easier than you think.

Tuscany has been largely spared from the commercial development that has popped up like weeds in Europe's asparagus patch. The bad news is that uninitiated travelers sometimes have difficulty finding accommodations outside the usual cities. The good news is that there are more rural rentals in Tuscany — from cottages to castles — than in any other part of Italy.

We selected our house — Casa Casina — from the catalog that we obtained from one of the rental agencies specializing in Italian properties. In addition to color pictures, the catalog provided a detailed description of the locale and the floor plan of the house including the number of bedrooms and baths and the fact that there was a television, central heating and a washing machine.

Our casa's location in central Tuscany, within walking distance of Cortona, gave us the advantages of a village to call "our own," as well as a convenient base for day trips to the surrounding countryside. We traveled in May, the prime time to see this land at its seductive best. In May, there is a lull in the seasons that makes Tuscany the

If You Go . . .

contessa of all Italian communi. The texture of her twilight is softer. The crinolines of her foliage crisper. Her pastels more tender. The wildflowers are in bloom, and the nighttime temperatures are warm enough to dine al fresco.

We flew to user-friendly Malpensa Airport in Milan, picked up the rental car (arranged through the house rental agency) and drove south to Santa Margherita. It was our first driving experience on the autostrade and we quickly learned to keep in the right-hand lane and out of the way of the Italian drivers whose speedometers seem to be calibrated in mach numbers.

After sleeping off our jet lag, we drove to Cortona, seeking out the back roads where traffic is lighter. The sleep-over and leisurely drive allowed us to arrive rested and ready for the rest of the day, which for weekly rentals, customarily begins at 3:00 P.M. on Saturday.

We found our house, a charming old stone two-story farmhouse that even came with its own hedgehog that lived in the garage. The beamed and plaster ceilings gave it a warm feeling of permanence. Downstairs was a living room with a fireplace, a well-equipped kitchen, a half-bath and a washer-dryer. Up the circular stairway were two bedrooms, one with a terrace and a full bath.

From the living room, French doors opened onto a stone patio bordered with potted geraniums and marguerites and a stone watering trough that had been used for centuries. Wild thyme and rosemary grew along the wall that bordered the lawn. Beyond the wall, the close-order drill of an olive orchard sloped away to the spired profile of Cortona and the broad plowed patchwork of the Val di Chiana.

Within a few minutes of our arrival, we were greeted by Rosa, our caretaker, who lived with her family in a farmhouse down the lane. She took us on a thorough tour of the house, pointing out the fuse box and the thermostat. When communication became too difficult for our Berlitz Italian, we compromised on French. Later she came over with fresh eggs and a homemade torta della nona.

Everything in the house worked as advertised. We once tripped the electric fuse when we overloaded the circuits — as we were warned not to do — by using the washing machine and a hair dryer at the same time, but the fuse box was convenient (be sure to locate it).

Our house was the perfect headquarters, close enough to Cortona for the convenience of it and far enough away to awake to the sound of birdsong, church bells and little else. When we weren't lounging and reading on the sunny terrace, we took compass-point daytrips to the surrounding area, either packing a picnic or seeking out a lunch of regional specialties at a local trattoria.

On one trip, we drove east into Umbria, as wooded and wild as New Hampshire. From Cortona, the narrow road, bordered with lilac, rose, wild pea, wisteria. iris and calla lilies, winds over densely forested hills of oak and chestnut to the medieval town of Gubbio. Stern and gray, it seems unlikely from its appearance that this somber, stone, hill town still produces the same colorful majolica pottery it introduced to the world in the sixteenth century. We circled through Perugia, stopping long enough to stock up on boxes of the famous chocolates made there, then returned to Cortona around the shores of Lake Trasemino, on whose shores Hannibal and his elephants routed the Roman legions in 217 BC,

Another day, we headed north to San Gimignano, Italy's best preserved medieval city with its fifteen fairyland towers — some over 150 feet tall — sprouting up from the village's one-eighth square mile area. We returned through castled Chianti country, along the strada del vino, leisurely exploring the ancient wine towns of Castellina, Rada, Greve and Gaiole.

South of Cortona, Tuscany looks exactly as you would expect. A day trip will take you over rolling hills striped with the butterscotch of plowed fields, past solitary chapels guarded by dagger-like cypress trees, to the castled hill town of Montepulciano, to the Renaissance order of Pienza, to the walled, hilltop village of Montalcino, inhabited since Etruscan times, where you can sample the local wines at an enoteca in the shadow of the fourteenth century castle keep.

To the west, across the Val di Chiana, the largest valley of the Apennines, is the unique medieval town of Lucignano with its stony, maze-like streets arranged like the concentric circles of a traditional

If You Go . . .

torta rustica. Nearby Monte San Savino, Santa Maria della Vertighe and the fortified village of Marciano della Chiana are some of the most beautiful and out-of-the-way towns in this part of Tuscany.

Perhaps the greatest pleasure of renting a house is having your own hometown. With a population of 22,000, Cortona is just the right size, small enough to get to know it and large enough for browsing and shopping and dining.

Some mornings we explored its narrow, flagstoned streets, passed chapels and quiet houses with wash in the windows and flowers on the stoop. More than once we wound our way up to the top of the town and the keep of the overgrown Medici fortress for a panoramic view of Lake Trasemino and the Tuscan countryside, one of the widest and finest views in Italy, or we walked the city's walled perimeter to marvel again at its four arched Romo-Etruscan gates.

We picnicked in the Gardino Publico, then in the evening followed families to restaurants we would have otherwise missed. We shopped with the local women for produce at the market under the arched portal of the Teatro Signorelli, bought postcards and Pinocchios and three-dollar bottles of Chianti along the Via Nazionale and had espresso and biscotti in the umbrellaed sun of the flag-draped Piazza della Republica.

Our evenings on the terrace were jealously guarded. It was time when we could just sit. Sit with a Campari and read in the last of the mellow, slanting light. Listen to the distant, evening bells of Cortona's thirteen churches and the forlorn cry of the cuckoo from the woods behind the house and smell the woody incense of the orchard's pruning fires.

If we felt like it, we went out for dinner. If not, we cooked, using the fresh produce we had bought in the market that day. And after dinner, we had coffee, biscotti and cherries soaked in Chianti on the dark terrace, listened to our tape of Andrea Bocelli and, 'til too late, talked and watched the stars.

Our only bad weather was the day before we left. At dawn, a cold rain began to drizzle from a low, gray sky. As I gassed up the car for the trip back to Milan, the attendant turned to me and said with a frown, "Bruto tempo." My dictionary Italian led me to believe that he was having a "bad time." It wasn't until he turned up his collar and scowled at the leaden sky I realized that by "bruto tempo" he meant the temperature was brutal. You've got to love a country where the word for time and temperature is the same.

On our last day, we settled up our account and said goodbye with hugs for Rosa and her family. They gave us cherries to take on our way. We promised to write. And we were gone. But not before we had reserved Casa Casina for the following spring.

If you go . . .

Getting There
Most major airlines fly to Rome and Milan. Tuscany is equidistant between the two airports. We chose the smaller Malpensa airport near Milan.

Accommodations
Some of the firms that arrange rentals are listed below. Many will arrange plane tickets and car rentals as well.

▲ The Parker Company 800-280-2811
▲ Rentals in Italy 800-726-6702
▲ Hideaways International 800-843-4433
▲ At Home Abroad 212-421-9165

▲ Ask if linens and towels are provided. Soap and toilet tissue are not. Europeans do not use face cloths so bring your own. Matches, salt, pepper and candles might come in handy.
▲ Electricity is AC but varies from 42 to 50 cycles and from 115 to 220 volts. Adapter plugs with two round prongs are required for American products.

If You Go . . .

▲ House rentals are by the week, usually beginning on Saturday at 3:00 P.M. and generally include insurance, water, and electricity. Heat might be extra. A deposit in Italian currency is often required on arrival.

Weather
Central Tuscany is temperate. In May, the average daily temperature is 60-65 degrees, and there are eight hours of sunshine. Rainfall in the month of May averages two inches. Avoid Easter, Liberation Day (April 25) and Labor Day (May 1).

Getting Around
▲ Car rentals are available at the airports. An International Driver's License is recommended and can be obtained from AAA, which can also arrange for traveler's health insurance. Italian roads are good, even the secondary ones. Take some Italian currency for the tolls on the autostrade. (Milan to Rome 25-30 euro).
▲ Service stations on the autostrade are open twenty-four hours a day hours, but any others are closed for two hours at lunch and few are open on Sunday or after 7:00 P.M. Not all take credit cards. The Automobile Club d'Italia (ACI) offers all motorists free roadside assistance by calling 116. The best maps are produced by ACI and are available at newsstands and bookstores. Tip: Autogrills are roadside restaurants at well marked intervals along the autostrade. Cafeteria-style food is good, fresh, cheap and favored by the locals. Also, an excellent selection of groceries, picnic supplies and wines and the restrooms are clean.

Shopping
Shop the markets for fresh produce. Tip: Do not touch the produce. The Italians are very sensitive about this. Point to what you want, and the merchant will select it. Shops close at noon, re-open at 2:00 P.M. and remain open until 7:00 P.M.

Food and Wine

Tuscan food is honest and hearty and the ingredients are always fresh. Regional specialties include crostini (thin slices of bread with pate), ribollita (a hearty vegetable soup), bistecca alla fiorentina (beefsteak cooked over coals), cinghiale (wild boar), papparardelle alla leper (wide pasta with stewed rabbit), and tagliatelle al fungi (pasta with mushrooms). Each region has its own wine, which complements the local dishes. Ask for it. Don't miss the vin santo, a delightful desert wine usually drunk with biscotti.

Dining Out

Cortona
- **La Logetta.** A converted wine cellar.
- **Tonino.** Local specialties.
- **Trattoria dell' Amico** and **Il Croce** for cheaper fare.
- **Miravalle** for the best views.

San Gimignano
- **Il Pino near the South Gate.** A good place to try the ribollita and the cinghiale. The local wine, La Vernaccia, is a good white.

Montalcino
- **Cucina de Edgardo.** Try the snails and polenta or the roast pork in balsamic and onions. The region's Brunello di Montalcino is one of Italy's best wines. This is a good place to try the pecorino, a local cheese made from sheep's milk.

Further Reading
- Mayes, Frances. *Under the Tuscan Sun.*
- Barzini, Luigi. *The Italians.*

Florence Off Season: An Unexpected Bargain

EVERY YEAR, HUNDREDS OF THOUSANDS OF TRAVELERS go to Florence to sample its culture and cuisine. The smart ones go off season.

In April it's warm enough to walk about, the madding crowds are far away, and, for the price of a ticket to a Broadway show, you can get a hotel room near the center of the city and some of the best food in the world.

Florence is a deceptively small town, and everything you will want to see and do is within a quarter-mile radius. The maze-like streets are easily walkable — no hills — and there is a pleasant surprise around every turn.

What To See and Do
You will need at least a week to see Florence. Anything less is a dizzying endurance test. The numerous museums, palaces and churches are striking examples of medieval and Renaissance architecture, and they contain more works of art than any city in Europe.

The first stop should be the Piazza del Duomo with its stunning trio of green, pink and white marble structures — the Gothic campanile, the sixteenth century baptistry with its gilded and paneled doors, and the massive church itself capped by the largest and most photogenic dome in the world. Don't miss the Museo dell' Opera del Duomo, one of Florence's finest, then linger with a technicolor gelato in the piazza where the echoing bombalating bells announce every quarter hour.

Florence Off Season: An Unexpected Bargain

Just north of the Duomo is the Galleria dell'Accademia which houses Michaelangelo's original David. (The others about town are copies.)

The Uffizi, on the Arno River, is Italy's finest art museum. The collections, arranged in chronological order from the thirteenth to the eighteenth centuries, are exhaustive and exhausting, so don't try to see it all in one day. The lines get long, so go early.

Adjacent to the Uffizi is the sunny Piazza della Signoria, dominated by the 300-foot tower of the Palazzo Vecchio. In front of the palace is another David, the fountain of Neptune, and the sculpture-filled Loggia della Signoria. Before you leave — whatever the time of day — stop at the Café Rivoire for a cup of hot chocolate you will never forget.

The Ponte Vecchio is just another street crowded with shops except for the views up and down the Arno from the double-sided belvedere in the center. Across the bridge is the Pitti Palace with its eight museums and the pruned and clipped meanderings of the Boboli Gardens. Also, on this side of the river, are the landmark frescoes of the Brancacci Chapel in the Santa Maria del Carmine and the Plaza Michelangelo, the best vantage point for a romantic and panoramic view of the city.

Have coffee and a bomboloni in the 1930s ambiance of the Café Gilli in the Piazza Repubblica. Don't miss the sculptures in the Bargelllo (seeing this old prison is worth the trip) and the nearby, surprising Orsanmichele, a granary turned chapel. Save time for Michelangelo's Medici chapels and the churches of Santa Maria Novella and Santa Croce — fine galleries in themselves. Some of the best art in the city is in the churches and it's free.

For a nice day trip, the forty-five-minute bus ride from Santa Maria Novella Station (bus #7) up to the tidy village of Fiesole for another classic panorama of Florence. Just below the village is a long Etruscan wall, which borders the remains of Roman temples and baths and an amphitheater, all well preserved.

If You Go . . .

Shopping in Florence

In addition to the chic boutiques along the Via Tournabuoni, Florence's busy streets and markets offer a variety of bargains. Perhaps the liveliest is the Mercato Centrale just north of the Duomo, where rows of open stalls sell everything from clothes to chianti. A must stop is the nearby glass and cast-iron food market, three floors of local produce, wine and cheese. The Mercato Nuovo, the old, covered Straw Market in the center of town, sells not only straw goods but also a variety of leather bags, linens and woodwork. Pet the snout of the bronze boar statue for good luck. By far the most fun is the Flea Market in the Piazza Ciompi with its irresistibly cluttered shops and sidewalk baskets overfilled with wonderful junk.

Where to Stay

Lodging in Florence can be a bargain. A number of small hotels within earshot of the Duomo bells have charming Old World rooms for as little as $80 a night.

▲ **Hotel Le Vigne in the Piazza Santa Maria Novella** — nineteen rooms — is in a nicely restored old building overlooking the piazza a few blocks from the Duomo in an area with a trattoria on every corner.

▲ **Hotel Porta Rossa,** built in the thirteenth century, is one of the oldest hotels in Italy. Minutes from the river and the Uffizi, the central location of this eighty-five-roomer is ideal.

▲ **Splendor,** not quite still splendid, but certainly satisfactory, the old building near Piazza San Marco resembles a grand mansion with antiques and frescoed ceilings.

▲ **Hermitage,** in a medieval building near the Ponte Vecchio, is one of the most popular hotels in Florence. Some of the rooms look out on the Arno.

▲ **Hotel Aprile** has twenty-nine rooms in a fifteenth century Medici palace near the Piazza Santa Maria Novella. There are numerous frescoes, a small bar and tearoom, and a courtyard garden where breakfast is served.

▲ **Pensione Annalena** is on a quiet street across the river near the Boboli Gardens and the Pitti Palace. This famous old pensione has twenty large rooms and a large garden

Where to Dine
Florence is a food town, and some of the best of it is found underground in its cave-like buca restaurants. Tucked away in the wine cellars of some of the city's grand old palazzos, these cozy subterranean trattorias, so beloved by the Florentines, offer Tuscan food at its finest at surprisingly good prices. The house wines are uniformly pleasant and compliment the hearty cuisine.

Although most numerous in the maze-like back streets of Florence's monument district, between the Ponte Vecchio and Santa Maria Novella, bucas can be found on both sides of the river. They are usually packed with regulars who always have reservations. For the Florentines, dining is an important event and not worth taking a chance on being disappointed. If you do not have a reservation, go at 7:00 P.M. and wait outside for the 7:30 P.M. opening.

▲ **Bucca Lapi** (Via del Trebbio 1R, telephone-231768) Founded in 1880, this bright and pleasant restaurant is in the old wine cellar under the elegant Palazzo Antinori. Vaulted ceilings arch over the dining tables and the open kitchen where chiefs turn out classic Tuscan fare. The owner patrols the tables, greeting guests and watching for any sign of dissatisfaction. Waiters present each dish with obvious pride, as if they had prepared it themselves, then stand by to see that it meets with your approval. The specialties include Tuscan bread and tomato soup, scampi gigantic alla garglia, fagioli toscani all'olio — Tuscan beans in native olive oil — bistecca fiorintina and pappardelle with chingale (wide noodles with boar). The duck with onions is memorable, as is the zucotto, a delicate liqueur-moistened pound cake filled with whipped cream, grated chocolate and nuts.

▲ **Buca Mario** (Piazza Ottaviani 16R, telephone- 214179) In business for a hundred years, this delightful buca in the arched wine cellar of the historic eighteenth century Palazzo Nicolini is one of the most famous cellar restaurants in Florence. In addition to an array of

If You Go . . .

homemade Florentine pastas, they offer beef carpaccio, grilled meats, chinghale with polenta and veal chop with truffle sauce — one of the showstoppers of the buca circuit. Save room for the poached pear with stewed prunes.

▲ **Buca delle' Orafo** (Via Volta dei Girolami 28R, telephone- 213619) A perennial favorite with Florentines who come for the home-style cooking, this friendly little buca, once part of a goldsmith shop, is under an arcade just off the Piazza del Pesce near the Ponte Vecchio. Featured dishes include mixed boiled meats with green sauce (olive, parsley, garlic, oil, capers and peas) and stracotto fagioli (beef braised in a sauce of red wine and vegetables), served with beans in a tomato sauce. Begin with the fennel-flavored salami and end with the sponge cake topped with almonds and meringue.

Although, strictly speaking, not true bucas, the trattorias listed below are among the most typical in Florence and have the same intimate atmosphere and solid Tuscan cooking.

▲ **Sostanza** (Via del Porcellana 25R, telephone- 212691) Hidden away in a canyon-like back street in the monument district, Sostanza is the city's oldest and most revered trattoria. The three friends who own and operate it have created a family atmosphere with long tables and pleasant service. As we waited outside for the doors to open, we could see inside the owners eating their own cooking. This is the place to try tripe — the Florentine way — cut into strips, then baked in a casserole with tomatoes, onions and parmesan cheese. For dessert have fresh strawberries with sugar and Chianti.

▲ **Belle Donne** (Via della Belle Donne 16R, telephone- 2382609) A favorite Florentine lunch place. Easily located by the crowd outside waiting to find a vacant seat at the closely packed marble topped tables. Check the blackboard inside below the window for daily home-style Tuscan specials. Start with the herring marinated in white wine and shallots or the traditional ribollita (a hearty vegetable soup with beans, cabbage, carrots and bread). The osso buco is a favorite, as is the asparagus Bismark with egg, so substantial it is listed with the entrees.

Florence Off Season: An Unexpected Bargain

▲ **Trattoria Garga** (Via del Moro 48-52, telephone — 239 8896) If you grow tired of the traditional Tuscan fare, check out some of the most creative cuisine in Florence. Tucked into the basement of a Renaissance building, this intimate little trattoria is decorated with lace curtains and bucolic murals. Featured dishes include tagliatelle with garlic, tomatoes, anchovies and smoked salmon; octopus with peppers and garlic; boar with juniper berries; spaghetti with blood orange slices, squid, shrimp and fresh tomato sauce; and the piece de resistance, tagliarini magnifico, made with angel hair pasta, orange and lemon rind, mint-flavored cream and Parmesan.

▲ **Angiolino** (Via Santa Spirito 36R) one of the many trattorias across the river and, for many, one of the most characteristic. The atmosphere is relaxed and homey with a stove in the center of the room and the open kitchen in full view. The food is pure Tuscan, featuring classic crostini, regional salumi, hearty soups and tripe. The specialty is penne ai funghi.

▲ **Trattoria San Augustino** (Via di San Augustino 287R)) Crowded into three cozy rooms, this trattoria's walls are lined floor to ceiling with a wide selection of wines to accompany your meal. Specialties include lamb cutlet with fried artichoke and one of the best dishes in Florence — risotto Gran Piscatore, a soupy, rich risotto covered with shrimp, oysters, calamari and mussels in the shell.

▲ **Latini** (Via dei Palchetti 6R) This noisy little trattoria is a neighborhood place where everyone seems to know each other. Dried hams hang from the ceiling and diners share Tuscan meals family-style at long tables. No reservations, so come early.

Meal Time

You won't need a watch in Florence. There is a natural rhythm to the day scored into neat three-hour measures which usually begin and end with eating. Start the day with coffee and a bomboloni — a créme filled donut — at the Danini bar in the sun-filled Piazza Della Repubblica. At midmorning, stop at the Café Rivoire in the Piazza Signori for a pastry and a cappuccino, or a cup of ultra-rich hot chocolate (you will need a spoon to get the last of it). Caught shopping at

IF YOU GO . . .

the Mercato Centrale at midday? Not to worry. On the Via San Casciano aisle on the ground floor (the aisles are named for nearby towns) is the Café Nerbone where you can get a classic boiled beef panino with green sauce and a gotino (shot glass) of chianti. Midafternoon is time for a technicolor cone of gelato, and to get you through that 5 o'clock valley of fatigue, duck into the Giacosa for a crostini and a Negroni — the classic cocktail of Campari, gin and red vermouth. Three more hours and it's time for dinner and then, to make room for breakfast, a walk down the Via Lungarno along the river filled with lights.

> **IF YOU GO . . .**
>
> Florence's Amerigo Vespucci Airport is served by Alitalia from Rome and Milan. The fifteen minute cab ride into the city is about fifteen euro. There is a train from Pisa (one hour) and Rome (two to three hours) which delivers you to Santa Maria Novella rail station near the heart of the city. You definitely will not need a car. There are no places to park, everything is close and walking is too much fun.

Western Sicily
An Island in a Sea of Light

SICILY IS THE ITALY OF ITALY. It is Italy writ large. Rustic, wild and hauntingly beautiful, this unspoiled island is a place of the senses, where everything Italian is magnified and intensified. The sun is brighter. The colors more vivid. The food zestier. The wine more muscular. The elegant decay more splendid. Here there is more dolce in the dolce vita. And yet, it is a place with a troubled history, steeped in myth, suspicion and legend.

Kicked off the toe of Italy like an unwanted triangular rock, Sicily sits at the crossroads of Europe and Africa. For centuries this largest of the Mediterranean islands was overrun and invaded by conquering outsiders, including the Greeks, Phoenicians, Romans, Goths, Arabs, Normans, Germans, French, Spanish and English. This cultural turmoil has left Sicily with a rich and varied culture manifest in the food and architecture and typified by a plaque on a church in Palermo inscribed in Greek and Latin and Arabic.

We got our first look at Sicily from a table on the terrace of a trattoria in Vila San Giovanni on the tip of Italy's southern coast. Rising abruptly from the sea as if angered, its mountainous bulk loomed in dark contrast over the four miles of peacock blue ink that filled the Straits of Messina separating it from the mainland.

We had driven down from Rome arriving late the day before. We planned to take the morning ferry and then drive to the western end of the island where we had rented a house on the sea. Without time to see all of Sicily's 10,000 square miles, we decided to concentrate on the less populated end of the island.

If You Go . . .

The trattoria where we sat was still run by the family of the man who founded it a hundred years ago to serve guests traveling by horseback. Our waiter was the grandson. He showed us a photograph of the mustachioed grandfather standing in front of the building in 1908 — the year that an earthquake flattened the building and the town and caused a tidal wave so high that fish were found in the mountains.

When we told him we were going to Sicily, he shrugged with resignation. "Then I will see you again next year. When you see Sicily, you will want to return."

Sicily is unexpectedly mountainous, especially at its eastern end. Expecting to find sun baked flats, we were surprised by the height of the almost continuous chain of mountains, covered with dense vegetation, piled along the coast and stretching back from the sea inland as far as we could see. Rows of pink and red and white oleander lined the highway and Jupiter's beard, poppies and bright saffron broom bloomed in the roadside ditches.

The sinuous, elevated highway, supported on long cement legs, wound through a series of villages where tile-roofed, terracotta towns clung to the hillsides. Plumes of white smoke rose from orderly olive orchards where sun-browned men burned the cuttings at small fires. Between the hills were glimpses of the broad sea and, over it all, the della robbia sky.

In contrast to the architecture of ancient Sicily which is varied and magnificent, modern Sicily is a land of unfinished projects, and this was nowhere more apparent than along the northeast coast. Everywhere cement buildings stood partially completed, sometimes with the ground floor occupied. As we drove into the country, we were struck by the contrast between the sweeping engineering of the autostrade draped gracefully over the mountains and the ruined and unfinished buildings that the road passed by.

As we drove west, the temperature rose with the mountain sun, drying out the land as we approached. The unkempt hilly verdure reminiscent of Tuscany gave way to the bare, stony white of Greece. In the small towns, men loitered in the shade and talked among themselves, watching us suspiciously as we passed.

The Sicilians have mastered the art of gesture, skillfully honing this pantomime into an art form. Nowhere, even in France, are the gestures more elaborate and more energetically displayed. Their meaning is so clear they can generally be understood by the uninitiated at first sight. After witnessing one of these artful demonstrations, we found ourselves stopping often for directions, even when we knew the way, just to watch the performance.

We found our apartment where the road ended at the sea. This charming Mediterranean villa is a series of connected white stucco apartments stacked down the face of a steep lava bluff, each with its own covered terrace to ensure privacy and an unobstructed view of the aquamarine Gulfo Castellammare and the mountains of the San Vito Peninsula twenty miles away.

The grounds were covered with flowering plants — mounds of geraniums, lantana, oleander, prickly pear, yucca, palms, iceplant, tamarisk, Queen Anne's lace and the wrought iron stalks of the century plant. A network of white cobblestone paths wound down the slope to a series of open terraces, each with a different view of the sea, ending at a paved niche where the water of a small blue private cove lapped at the lava grotto.

The shuttered doors and windows of our apartment opened directly onto the covered sea-view terrace. Inside the four tile-floored rooms, the plastered ceilings and walls were high and white. A ceiling fan rotated slowly overhead.

After unpacking, we drove along the coast through the nearby villages of Trappeto and Castellammare del Golfo, where a round-towered Aragonese castle guards the town and the scalloped beaches on either side. We stocked our kitchen at an outdoor market and then returned home to spend the afternoon with a Campari trying to decide which of the several terraces offered the best view of the sea and the sunset.

Dinner, prepared in our kitchen, was at twilight on the terrace — fresh seafood salad, tortellini with spinach and ricotta and fresh pomodoro, a salad of arugula and rosemary-infused oil the previous

If You Go . . .

guests had left on the counter and a lusty red Corvo which we bought at the market for four dollars.

The next morning we were awakened by the rhythmic hiss of the sea through the open window and the sounds of birds bickering in the trees just down the hill. We had breakfast on the terrace, then sat in the air-conditioned sunshine planning our day.

One thing you won't need in Sicily is a watch. There is a natural rhythm to the day as accurate and regular as the sun. The village mornings begin as the shops open at 9:00 A.M. Shopkeepers raise the shades and sweep the walks. Black-clad women with baskets begin their errands and noisy traffic crowds the streets. Church bells and the smell of fresh baked bread fill the air and men with their coffee talk in the sidewalk cafes. This is the time when the business of the day is done.

By 11:30, after a spectacular traffic jam, the streets are suddenly deserted. It is time for lunch. Shops are closed. People disappear from the streets, and the village goes quiet except for the sound of hushed voices and the clatter of plates from within the shuttered houses. It will remain this way until 4:00.

This is a good time to explore, when the traffic is light. But don't try to shop. Everything is closed, except for a rare bar for coffee and gelato. At this time of day, the country could be taken by a small squad of lightly armed men.

In a colorful market, we bought tomatoes still on the vine, blood oranges, purple onions and cherries. We wandered the streets of Terrasini, a warren of blocky, look-alike stucco houses with identical wrought-iron balconies and doorways draped with beaded curtains, which lent a distinct North African feel. At the foot of town, a perfect half-moon beach was backed by a fifty-foot wall of lava. Nearby, rows of brightly painted fishing boats bobbed along the stone quay. It was a perfect place for one of our many picnics.

At four o'clock, the village came suddenly alive. Streets that were previously empty filled with people of all ages. Couples strolled or stood embracing watching the sea. Old men, hands clasped behind their backs, walked the quay. Families, dressed as if for a wedding talked in groups, the children eating gelato. Young men gathered in groups to loiter in doorways, to preen and watch the girls pass. Dogs scampered among the umbrellaed tables at outdoor cafes. Music and laughter spilled from the doors and windows of the now-open bars. Cars, as if part of some holiday parade, lined the honking streets. Young men on motorbikes raced noisily about. As the twilight gathered, the pace slowed. People drifted from the streets into the restaurants. By 8:30, the restaurants are filled.

We had a typical Sicilian dinner at Orlando Furioso, a woody lofted trattoria where the waiters wore tuxedos and the owner's family dined at the next table. We began with white wine from Alcomo and a fresh seafood salad of calamari, shrimp, clams, octopus and mussels in lemon and oil, then spaghetti pomodoro, grilled swordfish and sea bass, followed by cassata, a sugary, iced ricotta cake topped with candied fruit.

The next day began clear and still. Across the Golfo, smooth as a summer lake, the tile-roofed geometry of the stucco villages tumbled down the hill to the water's edge like spilled blocks and lay in the slanting sun where they had fallen. Gulls mewed and swirled around two lone men in open fishing boats.

Our week of day trips began with a drive to Scopello, a picturesque, cobblestoned village with a central courtyard and a fountain that had grown up around an eighteenth century baglio, the manor house now occupied by a ceramic manufacturer. Below the village, wedged into a rocky niche is a pocket-sized turquoise harbor guarded by two Saracen towers. Stacked at the edge of the water, the abandoned, melon-colored buildings of a once-thriving tuna fishery decay in the sun. Rows of anchors lie in rusting ranks on the stone quay.

From Scopello, we drove to Erice, one of Italy's most beautiful medieval castle towns. Built by the eighth century Normans at the site of a Greek temple, it sits piled atop a 2000-foot volcanic plug overlooking the sea and the mountains of Capo San Vito. It is said that on a clear day, both the summit of Etna and Cape Bon in Tunisia can be seen from the walls of the city.

We picnicked in a small piazza in the shadow of a Norman cathedral and its square-sided campanile. Intricate checkerboard cob-

If You Go . . .

blestone stairs and streets of fitted stones led through the gray stone canyons of the old town, past imposing castles and decorative Arabian stone facades that hid, visible through open gates, cozy courtyards filled with flowers and cats. In the empty streets, some so narrow that only one person could pass, the eerie quiet for which this village is known was broken only by a group of lusty-voiced youths who passed singing "O Solo Mio."

From Erice the road winds down over ten miles of marbled and wildflowered hulls to Capo San Vito, a rocky fist of land thrust defiantly out into the sea. Nearby is the Zangara National Preserve, its plunging cliffs home to eagles, kestrels and falcons, which owes its pristine state to the Mafia who, for years, used its coves and beaches as smuggling bases. No cars are allowed in the preserve, but several walking paths crisscross its extraordinary landscape.

One morning we drove to Alcomo, on the slopes of Monte Bonafito, where vineyards produce one of the region's best white wines. The center of the small village is a long narrow piazza bounded by the Collegiate and Sant'Oliva, two of Alcomo's many fine churches.

We walked the narrow alleys, balconied with wrought iron, hung with flowers and drying wash. We seemed to be the only tourists, one of the things that pleased us about Alcomo. We bought an African rug from a merchant who gave us the name of a trattoria, which we later found with the help of a barber who left his shop, after retrieving his glasses, to point out the way through the maze of streets.

In Sicily there are more Greek temples than in all of Greece, and many are among the best preserved in the world. One of the most striking is the temple at Segesta. This temple with its thirty-six standing Doric columns was built in the twelfth century by refugees from Troy. Lonely and majestic, this tawny temple sits on the slope of a south-facing hill like a lion in the sun.

We wandered in awe through the roofless temple where swallows swirled among the pillars like wind-blown ash, then walked along the ruins of an ancient road, steps still in place, past ruins of walls and rooms to an almost complete amphitheater. Here we encountered another of the typical contrasts of Sicily. Through the worn stone ruins of the ancient theater, the view opened to the valley beyond where the modern grace of an elevated autostrade snaked its way over the farmlands.

Along the south coast, the ruins are more numerous, including the eight temples at Selinunte and the Valley of the Temples at Agrigento, the richest and most visited archaeological site in Sicily. We bypassed the crowded modern city and approached the temples from the south. There, spread for two miles across the Valley of the Temples, lie the remains of a dozen temples, tombs, sanctuaries and gates built in the fifth century B.C. Standing alone on a slight rise like a stone sentinel is the Temple of Concord, perhaps the best-preserved Greek temple in the world. Its thirty-four Doric columns, once coated with powdered marble and painted in bright colors, are now faded by centuries of sun to a warn, golden hue.

From Agrigento we drove back across the interior of the island, leaving the pale stuccos of the coastal towns for the gray, stone hill towns of the interior with their steep winding streets, wide enough at places for only one small car to pass. Broken peaks backed acres of rolling grassland patched with orderly plowed fields and the neat, well-tended rows of olive trees and vineyards. The narrow road wound over the wild empty land past the Mafia strongholds of Corleone and Prizzi, past the brooding cliffs of Ficuzza where, it is said, local dons forced their enemies to jump to their death on the rocks 1,400 feet below.

In Terrisini, we stopped for a lemon gelato so fresh it had a lemon seed in it. The owner, after living all over the world, had come back to buy a shop on the street where he was born. I asked him what he liked most about Sicily and, after thinking a minute, he said, " It has just enough of everything and not too much of anything."

In Sicily, there is a local saying. "Anyone who comes to Palermo without seeing Monreale arrives as a donkey and leaves as an ass." Situated in the mountains high above Palermo, the old city overlooks the Conca d'Oro and the sea. The central feature of the cobbled town is the cathedral, said to be one of the greatest works of Christian art. Built in 1172 by the Norman King William II, the upper half of the arched and pillared vault of the interior is covered by a

If You Go . . .

kaleidoscopic array of twelfth and thirteenth century gold leaf mosaics depicting scenes from the Bible. The mosaics cover 6,340 square meters, more than St. Mark's Square in Venice.

From Monreale, it is less than an hour's drive to Mondello. This fashionable seaside town, five miles west of Palermo, has a narrow horseshoe-shaped port and a perfect crescent beach. Gaily painted wooden boats line the quay and bob in water the color of blue gin. Shops and open-air trattoria line the one main street that borders the quay. Behind are neighborhoods and quiet streets of porticoed and balconied houses the color of melon and strawberry mousse with small, lush walled and gated gardens of hibiscus, lantana and bougainvillea.

Lunch at an umbrellaed trattoria was insalata di mare, spaghetti with baby clams, grilled sea bass and zuppa pescatore — the Sicilian version of paella with baby clams, calamari, whole sea bass, shrimp and mussels in a garlicky, oily broth stained with tomato and paprika served in a skillet with large, crisp croutons, perfectly accompanied by a white house wine. In the street, couples strolled or drove by with opera on the radio.

On the way back to the house we stopped at a pasticceria. We were alone except for the owner and his wife who proudly urged on us his almond cookies, ricotta-filled buns, pistachio cookies, rum babas and brioche filled with custard and stood by admiringly as we enjoyed them. When we asked if we could take his picture, he returned with his baker's hat and an ornately decorated ice cream cake and stood holding it at just the right angle to show it off. Captured in that one photograph is the Sicilian love of food, costume and ceremony.

We spent our last day sitting in the sun on our various terraces. After dinner, we sat in the perfect temperature of the Sicilian night, lit only by a three-quarter moon and a string of lights along the far shore of the gulf. From the owner's apartment, as if for our special benefit, a light breeze carried the strains of Andrea Bocelli's, "It's Time To Say Goodbye."

It was goodbye for now. But the waiter had been right. It is not possible to come to Sicily without wanting to return.

If you go . . .

Getting There

There are no direct flights to Sicily from the United States. Alitalia has frequent connecting flights from Rome and Milan. Ferries run from Genoa to Palermo (Gran Navi Veloci 010-589-331) and from Naples to Palermo (Tirrenia 091-602-1235). Book months in advance if you are taking a car. The drive from Rome to Villa San Giovanni on the autostrade takes all day. Car ferries to Sicily cross the Straits of Messina every twenty minutes around the clock. ($25)

Accommodations

Outside Palermo, hotels in western Sicily are scarce. The resort hotels of **Peria del Golfo** (091-8866-4770) and **Hotel Villaggio Citta del Mare** (091-868-7111) are near Terrisini. Further west, on the sea in Castellamarre, the **Hotel Al Madarig** has a restaurant and thirty-two rooms with baths.

Some of the firms renting houses and apartments are listed below:
▲ The Parker Company, 800-280-2811
▲ Rentals in Italy, 800-726-6702
▲ At Home Abroad, 212-421-9165

When To Go

Summer in Sicily can be very hot and very crowded. February, when the almonds bloom, through June, when it is warm enough to swim, are the best months to go. Temperatures in May average 75 degrees in the daytime and 60 at night.

If You Go . . .

Getting Around
A car is required to see western Sicily. Car rentals are available at the airport in Palermo. U.S. drivers are advised to have an International Driver's License (my U.S. license has always been satisfactory) which can be obtained through AAA, which can also arrange for your traveler's medical insurance. Sicilian highways, like those on the mainland, are excellent. Sicilians drive fast and take traffic lights and stop signs as suggestions. City streets are narrow and dangerous, especially in Palermo. The best time to travel is between 1:00 P.M. and 4:00 P.M. when the country comes to a halt for lunch.

Shopping
As in the rest of Italy, shops close at 1:00 P.M., reopen at 4:00 P.M. and close again at 7:00 P.M. Special purchases to consider: the fresh produce; colorful Sicilian pottery from Erice or Sant Stefano di Camastra; frazzata, colorful rugs woven in Erice; capers packed in salt, not vinegar, from the Aeolian Islands; Limoncello, a refreshing lemon liqueur and Marsala.

Food and Wine
Sicilian food is flavorful, zesty and always fresh. The variety and abundance of seafood seem endless. Regional specialties include pasta con sardi (fresh sardines, wild fennel, onions, tomato sauce, currants and pine nuts); involtini de pesce spada (thin slices of swordfish rolled around a stuffing of bread crumbs, olive oil, raisins, parmigiano cheese, onions, pine nuts and orange juice); spaghetti alle vongole (baby clams). The don't-miss-it street snacks are arancino (deep-fried breaded rice balls filled with tomato, meat and vegetable); panelle (fried squares of chickpeas); guasteddu,

or pani ca' muesa (a sesame roll filled with slices of spleen and caciocavallo cheese). The sweets are legendary — cannoli, cassata and gelato, the best ice cream in Italy. The wines are a perfect accompaniment to the bold foods. Try the red Corvo, or the whites from Alcomo.

Further Reading
DiLampedusa, Giuseppe. *The Leopard.* The classic historical novel of Sicily and its complex and troubled past.

The Dolomites: The Other Italy

IN ITALY'S MOUNTAINOUS NORTHEAST CORNER there are eighteen majestic peaks over 10,000 feet. This Italy can come as a surprise to the tourist expecting rolling hills, coastal flatlands and sun-splashed harbors.

Tucked away among the folds of these bright, sky-scraping Dolomites, the Val Gardena is a misplaced bit of Tyrol, where the shingle-roofed towns are freshly painted in Easter egg colors and the barns look like cuckoo clocks.

In the winter, the insiders come here to ski its surrounding ridges and high meadows. But in the summer, these highlands, covered with wildflowers, are a hikers paradise and, at a user-friendly altitude of 5,000 feet, the only thing breathtaking is the scenery.

We planned our trip for the June, after the skiers had gone and before the roads are filled with travel trailers and tour buses. The late spring days are sunny, the mountain wildflowers are beginning to bloom and the nights are warm enough to dine al fresco.

We flew to Milan, picked up our rental car and headed into the Alpi Orobie. As we wound our way north, the broad valleys and stone cottages of the hill country gave way to the white, brown-shuttered chalets of the Alto Adige, to sloped fields with smart yellow dandelions and vistas of snow-streaked crags Beyond Bolzano, we turned east into the Val Gardena and climbed to the village of St. Ulrich, named, for some reason, for the patron invoked against difficult births, dizziness, mice and moles.

THE DOLOMITES: THE OTHER ITALY

There is barely enough room in the narrow valley for the painted order of the little stucco town. The mountains are close and unavoidable. Beyond the pastel buildings, beyond the onion steeple of the church, beyond the sloping rim of obedient grassy meadows, spruce and larch forests rise quickly to the great, twisted pinnacles of the Dolomites, at this time of year still striped with snow.

Here, on the sunny side of the Alps, the ethnic inhabitants are Ladin, descendents of the Roman soldiers Emperor Tiberius sent to crush the Celts living in the mountain valleys of the Tyrol.

Since then, this prize of war has belonged successively to Austria, Germany and Italy and the culture still reflects that flux. The natives speak Ladin at home, German in the streets and the school children study Italian as a foreign language. One elderly woman we talked to said she had changed her nationality four times and had never left her village.

We found the old Hotel Stettneck, a welcoming, three-story butterscotch ten-roomer with balconies and brown shutters standing at the head of the main street a block from the sunny square. Owned and operated by the same family since 1913, the hotel everywhere reflects the attention given to making guests feel welcome, from the cozy lobby to the friendly dog in the foyer.

Our second-floor room was spacious and sunlit with parquet floors, painted wooden chests for the linens and a large featherbed. French doors opened onto a small balcony with table and chairs. From here we could survey the buildings of this alpine town of 4,500 which looked as if it had been painted yesterday. Across the street is the saffron Hotel Adler. The Hotel Posta on the corner is the color of strawberry yogurt, its annex a deep, delft blue.

We sat out the last of the cool sunshine with a cappuccino in the square, then had a typical Val Gardena dinner at Cucina Veneto, an eclectic dinner that began with antipasti and ended with strudel. In between there was lasagna with fontina, bean soup, wiener schnitzel, polenta, bratwurst and a local red wine. As we left, instead of the customary "Gratzie," our waiter thanked us with the linguistic mix, "Danke. Ciao."

If You Go . . .

The next morning, we awoke to the light on the silver peaks, the sound of birds in the garden and little else. For breakfast there was yogurt and eggs, fruit and muesli, the best bread of the trip, and a fruita d'bosca jelly made from alpine berries called mittilli, a cross between cranberries and blueberries and better than either.

We walked the maze of cobbled streets and shopped the tidy shops, window-boxed and trimmed with carved wooden gingerbread. For centuries, the people of St. Ulrich have specialized in woodcarving and there are said to be 3,000 woodcarvers in the valley. Shops are filled with carvings which vary in size from ten centimeters to ten feet. Some were natural wood, others smoothed and painted to look like ceramic. There were animals. Trolls and toys with moving parts. Angels and icons. Even a life-sized crèche, complete with chickens and eggs. St. Ulrich's church and museum have permanent collections of ancient and modern woodcarvings donated by local artists.

Aside from carving, the business of the village seemed to be maintenance. Never before have I seen a town so well cared for. Everywhere men were painting. For an hour I watched two men rebuilding a stone wall which had been damaged by a car. Working with a hammer and chisel, they carefully shaped each stone until it fit and held fast without mortar.

Shopkeepers swept their stores twice a day, at opening and closing. Street sweepers patrolled the streets even though there was nothing to sweep. Even the highways leading into town are swept. One night at 11:00 P.M., the manager of the hotel across the street was washing the sidewalk in front of the café.

We shopped for a picnic, bought cheese and bratwurst and whole-wheat rolls, and a great barbera (two dollars a bottle), which I found by following one of the natives to the supermarket wine rack. The wine was light and crisp and fruity, and we liked it so much that we came back later to get six bottles for the rest of our trip.

Over a craggy ridge just east of town lie the high meadows and plateaus of the Alpe di Siusi, a hiker's paradise, where we headed for the afternoon. The road to the Siusi winds around the ridge for fifteen miles through wooded and grassy slopes dotted with brown and

The Dolomites: The Other Italy

white chalets and neat farms with barns larger and more ornate than the houses. Sun dried and browned the color of Lincoln Logs, these precision-built barns' upper floors were tightly filled with firewood, trimmed and stacked like brown pencils.

The road passes through Kastleruth with its slender, square clock tower, through the farm village of St. Valentina to Siusi. Here the land opens up onto a great hummocky highland meadow, walled in on all sides by fractured gray spires and cliffs that rise half way to the vertical. The map indicates that the basin is eight miles long from crest to crest and equally wide, but the scale is so massive, it makes judgment of distance impossible.

We walked a path for an hour to the elevated plain where, nearly eye level with the peaks, the valley slopes away to the tender pastels of the distance. Leaving the footpath, we wandered out across the meadow, spongy underfoot and sprinkled with the colorful confetti of crocus and blue gentian. Rivulets of snowmelt trickled in their little ditches. We stopped at a wooden shack and had our picnic on a bench. To the north, the ice cream Alps of Austria glistened in the sun.

Our minds and cameras filled with images, we returned through the needled shade of larch and pine groves where gentian and heather bloomed on the boggy ground. We expected to see Heidi any minute. All that was missing was the soundtrack from "The Sound of Music."

After coffee and gelato at a sunny café, we soaked away the soreness in our spacious Italian tub and then sat on the balcony with a Campari and watched the shadows reclaim the slopes.

For dinner, we drove four miles back up into the mountains to Gasthof Panidersattel, a Swiss-style chalet with sunset views of the Val Gardena. The typical Tyrolean meal began with leberknodelsuppe (liver dumplings, or canederli) in a lemony broth, followed by herrengrostle, a savory skillet-cooked hash of potatoes, beef and onions topped with thin slices of speck (smoked pork), sauerbraten with mixed vegetables, fresh cabbage and horseradish salad and a bottle of Vernatch, a pleasing, light red wine that is the house wine of the area. There wasn't room for dessert, which would almost certainly have been apple strudel.

If You Go . . .

By then, we had enjoyed the area so much, we cancelled our trip to Cortina and extended our stay in St. Ulrich three more days.

The next day we took the car to St. Cristina, then up the steep one-track road to Monte Pana. A two-hour walk through spruce and mossed forest brought us to a high meadowland sloping away to the south. Behind us, patched with snow, the forbidding gray twins of the Grupo Sassolungo rose to 9,600 feet and seemed by their size alone to impose silence and reverence on the entire valley.

To the south the meadow fell away to the open grassy highland of the Siusi, where we had walked the day before, bounded on the west by the perfect cirque of the 7,500 foot Col di Puez and beyond that the snow-capped Austrian Alps. We had lunch of wine and cheese and barley rolls and braunschweiger and apples. Light showers, the only rain of the week, drove us to the dry security of a thick spruce tree where we sat on the antique roots and watched the clouds form and melt. It was windless, and there was no sound except for the forlorn cry of the cuckoo.

We returned to St. Ulrich for coffee in the sun of the Posta Café then had dinner at the Café Siveton: canderli suppe, spinach gnocci with cream and prosciutto, rump steak with gorgonzola, ice cream and fruiti de bosca.

For the next two days we hiked and picnicked the network of trails in the Siusi. The maps of the area are excellent, indicating the duration, length and degree of difficulty of each of the trails, none of which we found strenuous. Throughout the area, chairlifts, cog railways and gondolas operate in the summer to take hikers to the higher country.

We saved for another trip an overnight stay at one of the alpine refuges that are located conveniently along the mountain trails. Our first choice would have been the Refugio Bolzano di Monte Pez, one of the grand dames of the nineteenth century refuges.

Our last evening found us at the top of 7,500 Stella Pass, just north of town, where we had driven to watch the sunset. From here, the full range of the Dolomites was spread out before us, their limestone snags stained with the alpenglow of the setting sun. As we

The Dolomites: The Other Italy

relived out week, we agreed that the Val Gardena had surprised us. It wasn't the Italy we expected, but before leaving our hotel, we booked our room for the next year.

If you go . . .

Getting There
St. Ulrich (Ortisei) is in the Val Gardena, forty miles east of Bolzano. The nearest airports are in Milan, Verona and Innsbruck. Rental cars are available at all three.

Where to stay
▲ **Hotel Stettneck.** Delightful, family-owned and operated hotel with cozy rooms in the center of the village. Meals are available (0471-796563).
▲ **Aquila-Adler Hotel.** Glamorous accommodations with large garden and indoor pool and tennis court (0471-796203).
▲ **Ladinia.** Pleasant hotel with large rooms. Centrally located. (0471-796281).
▲ **Cendevaves.** In nearby Santa Cristina. Mountain views and indoor pool. (0471-796562).

The local tourist office has lists of hotels and rooms in private houses (0471-796328).

Where to dine
The food in the Val Gardena, like its history, is a blend of German and Italian. The bread is the best in Italy. Local specialties include canderli — dumplings flavored with smoked ham (speck) or liver served in soup or topped with cheese; grostle, a hash of potatoes, onions and meat. The region produces twenty wines, more DOC than any other region

If You Go . . .

in Italy. Try the white Muller Thurgan or the ubiquitous red, Santa Maddalena.

Typical regional meals are served at Cucina Veneto, Café Siveton, Janon and Gasthof Panidersattel in St. Ulrich and Freina in Santa Cristina.

When to go
Prices are highest and the area is most crowded from Christmas to Easter and from July to September

Hiking
The trails of the Alpe Siusi offer miles of classic alpine hikes. Access to the area is by way of numerous lifts from the Val Gardena or an auto road from the town of Siusi. Trails are well maintained, but suitable walking shoes are a must, as is a waterproof jacket. (Mountain showers can come quickly) No climbing skills are required. Trail maps are available at most hotels and at numerous branches of Assiociazione Guide Alpine. The best time for hiking is in the spring or fall. Mountain refuges are open from June to October.

Side Trips
Take the spectacular alpine loop over Passo di Gardena to Covera and return via Arrabo and Passo di Sella. Perhaps the grandest scenic drive in all of Europe is the Great Dolomite Road, a stunning one hundred forty-mile round trip from Bolzano to Cortina.